Better Homes and Gardens®

Microwave
Cook Book

On the cover: This assortment of micro-cooked recipes includes *Buttered Cranberry Punch, Pizza Joes, Easy Opera Fudge, Scotch Crunchies, Fruity Tapioca,* and *Golden-Sauced Franks.*

Above: Hard-cook the eggs on the range top while you micro-cook the potatoes and sauce. Then, assemble *Egg and Potato Casserole* and micro-heat. (See Index for page numbers.)

BETTER HOMES AND GARDENS® BOOKS

Editorial Director: Don Dooley
Managing Editor: Malcolm E. Robinson   Art Director: John Berg
Asst. Managing Editor: Lawrence D. Clayton   Asst. Art Director: Randall Yontz
Food Editor: Nancy Morton
Senior Food Editor: Joyce Trollope
Associate Editors: Rosemary C. Hutchinson, Sandra Granseth, Sharyl Heiken, Elizabeth Strait
Assistant Editors: Flora Elliott, Diane Nelson
Designers: Faith Berven, Candy Carleton, Harijs Priekulis

Contents

Our seal assures you that every recipe in the *Microwave Cook Book* is endorsed by the Better Homes and Gardens Test Kitchen. Each recipe is thoroughly tested for family appeal, practicality, and deliciousness.

At Home with Your Countertop Microwave Appliance

The day you brought your microwave oven home was a great occasion. With the user's manual in hand, you entered the world of micro-cooking. Perhaps boiling water for a cup of coffee or tea was your first experiment. Maybe you cooked bacon, baked a few potatoes, or baked some apples for dessert. Now that you have mastered those tasty beginnings, you want more time-saving recipes to prepare in this electronic cooking wonder. Look no farther. This cook book was written and the recipes were tested with your needs in mind.

How Foods Cook

You'll increase your enjoyment of the countertop microwave oven if you understand how this appliance cooks the food and why it is so different from conventional methods of cooking.

Conventionally: In your gas or electric oven you cook with hot air. The hot air cooks the surface of the food and the heat gradually works its way to the center of the food. By the time the food is heated all the way through, it is also brown on the outside. The heat of the air is regulated by a thermostatic control.

By microwave: By this new method of cooking, the food is cooked inside and out at the same time. For this reason, many quick-cooking foods do not brown—unless you use a browning unit.

The food cooks directly by means of electromagnetic energy similar to radio or light waves. The energy waves are called microwaves. These waves, traveling in straight lines, bounce off the walls of the oven cavity and are absorbed by the food. The microwaves cause the molecules in the food to vibrate and rub against one another. This rubbing or friction produces the heat simultaneously throughout the food.

You will notice that a standing time is sometimes specified in a recipe. This standing time, which comes after cooking in the microwave oven, allows for "carry-over" cooking. During this time, the heat spreads throughout the food, equalizing the temperature. To allow for carry-over cooking, it's occasionally necessary to slightly undercook the food.

Some recipes also specify to stir mixtures, turn dishes, and/or rearrange foods during cooking. One reason for this is that there is an uneven distribution of power in most microwave ovens. Another reason is that the waves lose power as they penetrate the food. Therefore, stirring a mixture is necessary to distribute the heated food. When stirring is not possible, turning the dish is a solution.

While microwaves are absorbed by food, they are reflected by metal and pass through glass, paper, china, pottery, and plastic. That's why the container you use for micro-cooking makes such a difference.

Micro-Cooking Utensils

Part of the fun of micro-cooking is the variety of containers you can use. There's no need to completely re-equip your kitchen just because you have a microwave oven. You'll be able to use many items already on your shelves. A basic rule of thumb is: glass, paper, and other containers that do not contain any metal are good. Metal blocks microwaves from doing their job. Under certain circumstances, some oven manufacturers allow a limited use of metal. Check the owner's manual for appropriate dishes to use in the model you have.

Also, consider the type of food you will be cooking and how long the food will be in the oven. Use dishes that withstand higher temperatures for foods containing high proportions of fats and sugars. You can use paper and certain plastic items for short-time cooking and for warming. For most other micro-cooking, use a dish that withstands hot food temperatures.

Dishes: Glass-ceramic and heat-resistant glass dishes, such as casseroles, baking dishes, bowls, measuring cups, and custard cups are especially satisfactory to use in the microwave oven. China without metal trim and dinnerware dishes can be used if recommended by the dish manufacturer or if they pass the dish test described in the tip box below.

Special microwave cookware: Microwave enthusiasts can buy non-metal cookware designed specifically for micro-cooking, including bacon and meat roasting racks, muffin pans, and fluted cake pans. (Follow manufacturer's directions for the proper use and care.)

Paper, wood, and baskets: For short-time cooking and simple cleanup, paper products are the answer. Cups, plates, napkins, and paper toweling are among the list of paper goods. Avoid using the wax-coated plates, cups, and bowls as cooking containers. The wax melts as the food gets hot. Wood and baskets should be used only for very short-time warming of food. They tend to dry out if they are in the microwave oven too long.

Covers: Not only does covering food keep moisture in and help heat food more evenly, but it also serves a safety function. Covers keep greasy foods from spattering and eventually clogging your oven's ventilating system. Use a glass lid, waxed paper, or clear plastic wrap to cover dishes. Plastic wrap is an excellent cover, but it must be vented to prevent a buildup of excess steam pressure. And waxed paper will act like a "partial cover," holding in heat but allowing some steam to escape.

Microwave Safety

Safe use of a microwave oven depends jointly on the manufacturer and the owner of the oven.

Manufacturer's part: Federal regulations specify safety features which must be built into the microwave oven.

Owners part: While the ovens are built with safety in mind, microwave safety also depends on how you care for the appliance. Read the instruction book for operation techniques and special cautions, as these directions may vary from oven to oven.

Examine the oven. If the door doesn't close properly or if there is any damage to the door hinge, latch, or sealing surface, don't operate the oven. Have it corrected by a qualified service person. Also, don't operate the oven if an object is caught in the door and don't insert objects through the door seal or the oven vents. To ensure safety, do not tamper with the interlocks or the high voltage connection, and don't lift the oven using the door as a handle.

Dish Test

To test whether a dish is suitable for use in a microwave oven, make the following test: Pour ½ cup cold water into a glass measure. Set measuring cup inside the dish to be tested. Micro-cook 1 minute.

Use: If water is warm and dish remains cool, or if dish is warm yet can still be picked up with bare hands, the dish can be used.

Do not use: If water remains cool and dish gets too hot to handle, do not use for micro-cooking.

Keep the oven clean. Frequently clean the cavity, door, and the door seal with water and a mild detergent to keep the oven free from food spatters, especially grease.

Other safety tips: Do not pop corn in the microwave oven. The small amount of corn that's used for popping doesn't absorb enough energy to pop. There's an additional hazard to the container; a paper bag could catch fire and a glass dish could get too hot and break.

Also, don't cook eggs in the shell or bake potatoes without pricking the skin. The steam pressure can build up inside the eggshell or potato skin and the egg or potato can explode.

Timings for Micro-Cooking

Several variables affect the cooking times of foods prepared in a microwave oven. For instance, house voltage may be high or low. Other variables can be grouped into two major categories, the oven itself and the food to be cooked in the appliance.

Ovens: Brands of ovens vary by model and by manufacturer. They also produce different amounts of cooking power. Therefore, the timings given in recipes are approximate to allow for various models. (See tip box for information regarding recipe timings.)

Food: Micro-cooking times also depend on the characteristics of the food to be cooked. Some of these characteristics are:

1. Beginning temperature—foods just out of the refrigerator take longer to heat than room temperature foods.

2. Size and shape—small foods cook faster than large items. Regular-shaped foods heat more evenly than irregularly shaped foods. Thin foods cook more quickly than thicker foods.

3. Density—porous foods micro-cook faster than more compact and solid food items.

4. Quantity—the more food being cooked at one time, the longer the food will take to cook. Remember this when you're thinking about doubling a recipe. It's better to cook in smaller batches and repeat the cooking procedure rather than to cook a large quantity at once.

5. Browning—certain foods don't brown when micro-cooked. Although some people consider the lack of browning a drawback, actually it isn't. It's just that we are accustomed to seeing foods with a browned appearance. A good example are cupcakes which are to be frosted. Once the frosting is spread on the cakes, no one knows whether or not the surface was browned during baking.

Solutions: Use doneness tests as your guide when micro-cooking. The golden rule for microwave cooking is "cook and look." Learn to judge the degree of doneness for the various types of foods that you micro-cook.

If browning is an important part of the recipe, or is important to you, there are several suggestions: brown the food under the conventional broiler; brush meats lightly with Kitchen Bouquet; or, sprinkle some main dishes lightly with paprika. A crumb topping can also enhance the appearance of the food.

Recipe Timings

Recipes in this book were tested in countertop microwave ovens operating on 2,450 MHz (megaHertz) frequency. Unless specified otherwise, the high or cook setting was used. The manufacturer's power output rating of the ovens used in testing ranged from 600 to 700 watts. The literature which comes with your oven should tell you the wattage output rating. Or, ask the local dealer.

Less than 600 watts: Foods cooked in ovens with less wattage output may need extra cooking time. First, check the food for doneness at the timings given. Then add more time, checking after every 30 seconds to avoid overcooking.

More than 700 watts: Foods cooked in ovens with higher wattage output may need less cooking time. Check foods for doneness a little sooner than timings listed in the recipes.

Or, if available, use the browning unit of the microwave oven or the special microwave browning dish.

Special Uses for the Oven

Use your microwave appliance for many cooking tasks normally done on top of the range and also for some of those jobs done in your regular oven. Besides general recipe preparation, popular uses for the microwave oven include the quick reheating of leftovers, take-out foods, and convenience foods, plus the speedy thawing of frozen foods.

Leftovers: In these days of stretching the dollar, it's important to use up every bit of food. The microwave oven makes turning leftovers into a meal a snap. The food is palatable and easy to serve. As a general guideline for reheating cooked food, allow about 1½ minutes for each cup or 8 ounces of cooked food. When warming several different foods on one plate, make sure that the serving portions are similar for even heating. It's a good idea to underheat the food and check the temperature before continuing to cook.

Convenience foods: Turn the supper you purchased at the deli on the way home into a warm-as-toast meal with your microwave oven. There are many other convenience foods you can heat in your oven, too. However, check the oven manufacturer's directions for products and timings for these foods as well as whether you can cook food in its foil pan.

Defrosting foods: If you've ever been caught having to prepare dinner but have forgotten to take some food out of the freezer to thaw, you'll certainly appreciate a microwave oven. The frozen food is thawed, cooked or heated, and ready for your hungry family in practically no time at all.

Some models have a defrost setting as a built-in feature. If your appliance has an automatic defrost, consult the manufacturer's directions for usage instructions and for timings.

However, defrosting can be done in any microwave appliance without an automatic defrost. Simply alternate cooking and standing times. The standing time allows the food temperature to equalize so that the outside of the food doesn't begin to cook while the inside of the food is still defrosting.

As rule of thumb, for every 1 cup or 8 ounces of frozen, cooked food, micro-cook 1 minute and let the food stand in the appliance without the power turned on for 1 minute. Repeat the cycles until just a few ice crystals remain in the food. For 2 cups or 16 ounces, the cycles would be 2 minutes on, 2 minutes off. Once the food is thawed, micro-heat allowing about 1½ minutes per cup of food. Follow recipe directions for preparing uncooked frozen food.

Other uses: Not only do you use your oven to prepare entire recipes, you also will use it to do those small tasks, such as melting butter or chocolate for cooking. Or, you can get crisp bacon for a bacon-lettuce-and-tomato sandwich by cooking slices between layers of paper toweling in a flat dish. Merely allow 1 to 1½ minutes for one slice; 2½ to 3 minutes for four slices; and about 4½ minutes for six bacon slices. Or, for a quick snack that even the kids can fix, wrap a frankfurter and frozen bun together in a paper napkin and micro-cook in less than a minute.

As you use your microwave appliance, you will undoubtedly find many other uses that will help you with everyday food preparation chores. You may even discover some non-food uses for the oven.

Converting a Recipe Favorite

Converting recipes takes some experimenting. To avoid boil overs, you may need a larger baking dish than specified in the conventional recipe. Start checking food for doneness after approximately one-fourth of the conventional cooking time. Then, continue cooking, checking the food often, until it's done. Or, use a similar recipe in this book as a guideline.

Tantalizing Microwave Recipes

Cooking has come a long way since the black pot and open fire of yesteryear. Today's and tomorrow's foods cook electronically in a fun-to-use microwave oven. It simplifies and shortens cooking chores so that you, the cook, have more time to spend with family and friends. There are so many different and tantalizing foods you'll want to try in your microwave oven. Just look through the following section for a wide array of recipes, from snacks, appetizers, main dishes, and vegetables, to tempting desserts and candies.

Use cooking times as guidelines since countertop microwave ovens vary by manufacturer. See tip box on page 6 for information regarding recipe timings.

This trio of main dishes is just a sampling of the great tasting recipes prepared in the microwave oven. Choose from *Oriental Beef Ring, Peach-Glazed Spareribs,* or crumb-topped *Turkey-Spinach-Rice Bake.* (See Index for page numbers.)

Appetizers, Snacks, and Beverages

Looking for party-style appetizers or snacks and beverages for spur-of-the-moment treats? Then glance over the next few pages for some tempting recipes to suit the occasion. You'll see that the microwave oven is one of the easiest appliances to use for preparing those between-meal, short-order foods.

Peppy Almonds

  2 tablespoons butter *or* margarine
1½ teaspoons chili powder
  1 teaspoon celery salt
  1 teaspoon Worcestershire sauce
  ½ teaspoon salt
  ⅛ teaspoon cayenne
1½ cups whole almonds (8 ounces)

In a 10x6x2-inch baking dish micro-melt the butter or margarine 30 to 40 seconds. Stir in chili powder, celery salt, Worcestershire sauce, salt, and cayenne. Add almonds; stir to coat. Micro-cook, uncovered, about 7 minutes, stirring twice. Cool thoroughly on paper toweling. Makes 1½ cups nuts.

Parmesan Nibble Squares

Cereal takes on a new character. Use either rice or corn squares as your fancy dictates—

  2 tablespoons butter *or* margarine
  ⅛ teaspoon garlic powder*
  2 cups bite-size shredded rice
    or shredded corn squares
  ¼ cup grated Parmesan cheese*

In a 10x6x2-inch baking dish combine butter and garlic powder. Micro-melt the butter 30 to 40 seconds. Stir in rice or corn squares till coated with butter mixture. Sprinkle with cheese. Micro-cook, uncovered, about 3 minutes, stirring twice. Cool. Makes 2 cups.

  Note: If desired, substitute ⅛ teaspoon paprika for the garlic powder and 3 tablespoons grated American cheese food for the grated Parmesan cheese specified in recipe.

Clam Dip

  2 slices bacon
  1 8-ounce package cream cheese
  ¼ cup finely chopped onion
  2 tablespoons grated Parmesan cheese
  2 tablespoons chili sauce
  2 tablespoons milk
  ½ teaspoon dried basil, crushed
  ¼ teaspoon garlic salt
  ⅛ teaspoon pepper
      ● ● ●
  1 7½-ounce can minced clams
    Crackers and vegetable dippers

In a 1-quart casserole place bacon slices between layers of paper toweling. Micro-cook until bacon is crisp, about 2 minutes. Remove bacon and paper toweling; crumble bacon and set aside. Place cream cheese in same casserole. Micro-cook, covered, just till softened, about 1 minute. Blend in onion, grated Parmesan, chili sauce, milk, basil, garlic salt, and pepper. Drain clams. Stir drained clams into cheese mixture. Micro-cook, uncovered, until heated through, about 3 minutes, stirring after each minute. Stir in crumbled bacon. Serve warm with crackers and vegetable dippers. Makes 1⅔ cups dip.

Toasted Pumpkin Seeds

In a 10x6x2-inch baking dish combine 2 cups raw unprocessed shelled pumpkin seeds (8 ounces), 1 tablespoon cooking oil, and 1½ teaspoons salt *or* 1½ teaspoons seasoned salt *or* 1 teaspoon garlic salt. Micro-cook, uncovered, 8 minutes, stirring every 2 minutes. Cool thoroughly on paper toweling. Store in tightly covered container. Makes 2 cups.

The next time you have a party, try one or more ▸ of these quick-to-fix snacks—*Taco Chicken Wings, Peppy Almonds, Clam Dip,* or *Hot Buttered Lemonade.* (See Index for page numbers.)

Garlic Bean Dip

Save dish-washing by cooking the bacon and the dip in the same casserole—

>   **2 slices bacon, chopped**
>   **1 8-ounce can red kidney beans,
>   drained**
>   **¾ teaspoon chili powder**
>   **½ teaspoon onion salt**
>   **⅛ teaspoon garlic powder**
>   **Dash pepper**
> **• • •**
>   **¾ cup dairy sour cream**
>   **Corn chips *or* tortilla chips**

In 1-quart casserole place bacon. Cover with paper toweling. Micro-cook till bacon is crisp, about 2 minutes. Remove bacon and paper toweling, leaving any drippings in casserole.

To bacon drippings in casserole add the drained kidney beans, chili powder, onion salt, garlic powder, and pepper. Mash the beans till smooth; blend with the seasonings and drippings. Micro-cook, covered, till mixture is heated through, about 1 minute. Fold in the dairy sour cream and crisp-cooked bacon. Micro-cook, uncovered, just till hot, about 2 minutes, stirring every 30 seconds. Serve the dip warm with chips. Makes 1¼ cups dip.

Zesty Cheese Dip

Horseradish and mustard add zip—

>   **1 8-ounce package cream cheese**
>   **1 5-ounce jar sharp American
>   cheese spread**
> **• • •**
>   **⅓ cup beer**
>   **1 tablespoon snipped green onion
>   tops**
>   **½ teaspoon prepared horseradish**
>   **¼ teaspoon dry mustard**
>   **Crackers and vegetable dippers**

In a 1-quart casserole combine the cream cheese and sharp American cheese spread. Micro-cook, covered, just till softened, about 1 minute. By hand, gradually beat in the beer, onion, prepared horseradish, and dry mustard till smooth. Micro-cook, covered, until heated through, about 3 to 3½ minutes, stirring after each minute. Stir before serving. Serve warm with crackers and vegetables. Makes 1¾ cups.

Teriyaki Appetizer Meatballs

>   **2 beaten eggs**
>   **⅓ cup milk**
>   **⅓ cup fine dry bread crumbs**
>   **2 tablespoons finely chopped onion**
>   **½ teaspoon salt**
>   **⅛ teaspoon pepper**
>   **1½ pounds ground beef**
>   **4 teaspoons cornstarch**
>   **1½ teaspoons sugar**
>   **½ teaspoon ground ginger**
>   **¾ cup beef broth**
>   **3 tablespoons soy sauce**
>   **1 tablespoon dry sherry**
>   **1 clove garlic, crushed**

In mixing bowl combine eggs, milk, crumbs, onion, salt, and pepper. Add beef; mix well. Shape mixture into 48 meatballs; set aside. In a 2-cup glass measure blend cornstarch, sugar, and ginger. Stir in broth, soy, sherry, garlic, and ¾ cup water. Micro-cook, uncovered, till hot, about 3 to 4 minutes. Stir. Micro-cook, uncovered, till thickened and bubbly, 1 to 2 minutes more, stirring every 30 seconds. Transfer to blazer pan of chafing dish and place over hot water. Arrange *24* of the meatballs in 12x7½x2-inch baking dish. Micro-cook, covered, till meatballs are done, about 4 minutes, rearranging meatballs during cooking. Remove meatballs from dish with slotted spoon and add to hot sauce in chafing dish. Repeat with remaining meatballs. Serve with wooden picks. Makes 48 appetizers.

Taco Chicken Wings

These "drumsticks" are shown on page 11—

>   **1½ pounds chicken wings (8)**
>   **Milk**
>   **2 tablespoons taco seasoning mix**
>   **2 tablespoons fine dry bread
>   crumbs**

Remove wing tips and discard; separate wings at joints. Dip chicken pieces in milk. Combine seasoning mix and bread crumbs in plastic bag. Add two or three chicken pieces at a time, shaking to coat. Place chicken in 12x7½x2-inch baking dish. Micro-cook, covered, till chicken is done, about 14 minutes, giving dish half turns every 4 minutes. Makes 16.

Appetizer Franks

1 8-ounce can tomato sauce
½ cup water
2 tablespoons vinegar
1 envelope spaghetti sauce mix
1 tablespoon sugar
¼ teaspoon dry mustard
1 pound frankfurters, cut in
    bite-size pieces

In 2-quart casserole combine the first 6 ingredients; stir in franks till coated. Micro-cook, covered, till heated through, about 7 to 8 minutes, stirring twice. Keep warm in chafing dish. Serve with wooden picks. Makes about 36.

Scallop Kabob Appetizers

1 12-ounce package frozen scallops
2 tablespoons snipped parsley
2 tablespoons cooking oil
2 tablespoons lemon juice
2 tablespoons soy sauce
½ teaspoon salt
    Dash pepper
12 slices bacon, cut in
    thirds crosswise
1 6-ounce can whole
    mushrooms, drained
1 20-ounce can pineapple
    chunks, drained

Remove frozen scallops from package (35 to 40). To thaw, place in 12x7½x2-inch baking dish. Micro-cook, covered, 1½ minutes, stirring twice. Rinse scallops; drain. Combine next 6 ingredients; add scallops. Let stand 1 hour at room temperature; stir occasionally.

Meanwhile, partially cook bacon by placing two layers of paper toweling in 12x7½x2-inch baking dish. Add *half* of the bacon; cover with paper toweling. Micro-cook 3½ minutes. Drain on additional paper toweling. Repeat with remaining bacon. Remove scallops from marinade. For each kabob, thread a scallop, mushroom, piece of bacon, and pineapple chunk on a wooden pick. Place *half* the kabobs in a 12x7½x2-inch baking dish. Micro-cook, uncovered, for 8 minutes, giving dish a half turn every 2 minutes and brushing kabobs with marinade. Repeat with remaining ingredients. Serve warm. Makes 35 to 40 appetizers.

Blue Cheese-Stuffed Mushrooms

24 fresh mushrooms, each about 1 inch
    in diameter (1 pound)
1 tablespoon butter *or* margarine
⅓ cup crumbled blue cheese
3 tablespoons fine dry bread
    crumbs
¼ cup snipped parsley

Remove stems from mushrooms; set caps aside. Chop stems. In 2-cup glass measure combine butter and stems. Micro-cook, uncovered, till tender, about 2 minutes; stir once. Stir in cheese and crumbs. Spoon about *1 teaspoon* filling into *each* mushroom cap; sprinkle with parsley. Place 12 filled mushrooms in a glass pie plate; micro-cook, covered, till hot, about 2 minutes, turning dish once. Cook remaining mushrooms. Makes 24.

Seafood Appetizers

1 4½-ounce can shrimp, drained and
    mashed *or* 1 6½- or 7-ounce can
    tuna, drained and flaked
¼ cup mayonnaise *or* salad dressing
2 tablespoons chili sauce
1 tablespoon finely chopped celery
1 tablespoon finely chopped onion
32 rich round crackers

Combine shrimp or tuna and next 4 ingredients; spread about ½ *tablespoon* mixture on *each* cracker. Place *eight* of the appetizers at a time on a paper plate. Micro-cook, uncovered, till hot, about 30 seconds. Trim with parsley, if desired. Serve immediately. Makes 32.

Nachos

Cut 2 ounces Cheddar *or* Monterey Jack cheese into twenty-four ¾-inch squares, each about ⅛ inch thick. Dice 1 canned mild chili pepper. Arrange 12 taco-flavored tortilla chips on a plate. Using ½ cup canned bean dip, top *each* chip with *1 teaspoon* of the bean dip, a piece of chili pepper, and a piece of cheese. Micro-cook, uncovered, just till cheese melts, about 30 to 45 seconds, turning plate several times. Repeat with 12 additional chips and remaining dip, pepper, and cheese. Makes 24.

Salami-Bean Appetizers

    1 8-ounce can pork and beans in
        tomato sauce
    1 medium dill pickle, cut up
    1 tablespoon prepared mustard
    8 ounces salami, cut in pieces
    64 rich round crackers

Combine pork and beans, cut up dill pickle, and mustard in blender container. Blend till combined. With blender running, add salami pieces, a few at a time, blending till well combined. (Occasionally stop blender and use rubber spatula to scrape down sides of container.) Spread about ½ *tablespoon* of the mixture on *each* cracker. Trim with chopped dill pickle, if desired. Place *16* of the crackers on a paper plate on paper toweling. Micro-cook, uncovered, till hot, about 1 minute. Serve at once. Repeat three more times. Makes 64.

Buttered Cranberry Punch

A colorful beverage shown on the cover—

    3 cups cranberry-apple juice
        drink
    ¼ cup packed brown sugar
    ¼ cup orange juice
    3 tablespoons lemon juice
    4 inches stick cinnamon
        Butter *or* margarine

In a 1½-quart casserole or heat-proof pitcher combine the first 5 ingredients. Micro-cook, uncovered, till almost boiling, about 8 to 9 minutes. Remove cinnamon. Serve in mugs. Top *each* serving with about *1 teaspoon* butter. Makes 4 (7-ounce) servings.

Hot Vegetable Cocktail

    2 12-ounce cans vegetable juice
        cocktail (3 cups)
    2 teaspoons lemon juice
    1 teaspoon Worcestershire sauce
        Dried dillweed

In 4-cup glass measure combine vegetable cocktail, lemon juice, and Worcestershire. Micro-cook, uncovered, till hot, 5 to 6 minutes, stirring twice. Serve in mugs. Sprinkle with dillweed. Makes 6 (4-ounce) servings.

Coffee Plus

    2 cups water
    3 tablespoons coffee liqueur
    2 tablespoons instant coffee
        crystals
    2 tablespoons crème de cacao
    1 tablespoon brandy
        Whipped cream
    4 cinnamon sticks (optional)

Combine water, coffee liqueur, coffee crystals, crème de cacao, and brandy. Pour into four coffee cups or mugs. Arrange cups in micro-wave oven. Micro-cook, uncovered, until liquid is heated through but not boiling, about 4½ minutes. Top each serving with a dollop of whipped cream. If desired, serve with cinnamon stick stirrers. Makes 4 (4-ounce) servings.

Chocolate Coffee

    ½ cup sweetened cocoa mix
    4 teaspoons instant coffee
        crystals
    3½ cups water

In a 4-cup glass measure combine sweetened cocoa mix and instant coffee crystals. Blend in enough of the water to dissolve sweetened cocoa mix and coffee crystals. Stir in the remaining water. Micro-cook, uncovered, till mixture boils, about 7 to 8 minutes. Stir well. Serve in mugs. Makes 4 (6-ounce) servings.

Easy Instant Coffee

Making coffee in the microwave oven is a breeze. For 8-ounce mugs, combine about 1 teaspoon instant coffee crystals in each mug with ¾ cup water. Micro-cook just till hot: 1 mug—1¼ minutes; 2 mugs—2 minutes; 4 mugs—3½ minutes.

For larger mugs, combine coffee crystals (about 1¼ teaspoons) in mug with 1 cup water. Micro-cook just till hot: 1 mug—1½ minutes; 2 mugs—2½ minutes; 4 mugs—4¾ minutes.

Spiced Honeyed Cider

In a 4-cup glass measure mix 3 cups apple cider *or* apple juice, 1 tablespoon honey, ¼ teaspoon ground cinnamon, and ⅛ teaspoon ground nutmeg. Micro-cook, uncovered, till hot, about 6 to 7 minutes. Serve in mugs. Dot with butter. Makes 4 (6-ounce) servings.

Hot Buttered Lemonade

Good on wintry days; shown on page 11—

  ½ cup sugar
  6 inches stick cinnamon
  6 whole allspice
  4 whole cloves
  ½ cup lemon juice
  3 tablespoons brandy *or* rum
    (optional)
  Butter *or* margarine

In a 4-cup glass measure combine sugar and 2 cups water. Loosely tie spices in cheesecloth; add to sugar mixture. Micro-cook, uncovered, till boiling, about 6 to 7 minutes. Let stand 30 minutes. Stir in lemon juice. Micro-cook till boiling, 6 to 7 minutes longer. Remove spice bag. Stir in brandy or rum, if desired. Serve in mugs. Top *each* serving with about *1 teaspoon* butter. Serve with cinnamon stick stirrers, if desired. Makes 4 (6-ounce) servings.

Tomato Tune-Up

  3 cups tomato juice
  1 10½-ounce can condensed beef
    broth
  ½ cup sliced celery
  ⅓ cup dry white wine (optional)
  2 thin onion slices
  1 bay leaf
  4 whole cloves
  Bottled hot pepper sauce
  4 thin lemon slices, halved

In a 2-quart casserole combine tomato juice, beef broth, celery, wine, onion, bay leaf, cloves, and several dashes hot pepper sauce. Micro-cook, covered, till boiling, about 10 minutes, stirring twice. Strain soup; serve in mugs or small bowls. Float a halved lemon slice in each. Makes 8 (4-ounce) servings.

Hot Chocolate Malted

  1 pint vanilla ice cream
  ¾ cup milk
  ¼ cup chocolate-flavored syrup
  1 tablespoon instant malted
    milk powder

Place all ingredients in a 4-cup glass measure. Micro-cook, uncovered, till hot, about 5 to 6 minutes, stirring twice to melt ice cream. Serve in mugs. Makes 4 (4-ounce) servings.

Peanut-Mallow Smoothy

  ¼ cup creamy peanut butter
  ¼ cup butterscotch topping
  2 cups milk
  Marshmallows

In a 4-cup glass measure blend peanut butter and butterscotch topping; gradually stir in milk. Micro-cook, uncovered, 6 minutes, stirring every 2 minutes. Beat with rotary beater till smooth. Pour into mugs. Top with a marshmallow. Makes 4 (4-ounce) servings.

Eggnog Special

  4 cups milk
  ¼ cup sugar
  1 teaspoon vanilla
  ¼ teaspoon salt
  2 beaten eggs
  1 beaten egg yolk
  1 egg white
  ½ teaspoon vanilla
  2 tablespoons sugar
  Ground nutmeg

In a 2-quart heat-proof pitcher or bowl combine milk, ¼ cup sugar, 1 teaspoon vanilla, and salt. Micro-cook, uncovered, till hot, about 8 minutes. Stir. Combine eggs and egg yolk. Gradually stir *1 cup* of the hot mixture into beaten egg mixture. Return to hot mixture. Micro-cook, uncovered, 2 minutes more, stirring once. Beat egg white and ½ teaspoon vanilla till soft peaks form; gradually add the 2 tablespoons sugar, beating to stiff peaks. Pour eggnog into mugs. Top with small dollops of the egg white mixture. Sprinkle with nutmeg. Makes 8 (4-ounce) servings.

Main Dishes for Moderns

*L*et your microwave appliance speed up the preparation of the main course. In this section, you'll find an assortment of seafood, poultry, and meat main dishes—recipes that are perfect to serve for either family or company meals.

Elegant Fish Roll-Ups

      2 pounds fresh or frozen
          flounder fillets
        Salt
    ¼ cup chopped onion
    1 tablespoon butter *or* margarine
    1 7¾-ounce can salmon, drained,
          bones and skin removed, and
          flaked
    2 tablespoons snipped parsley
        Dash pepper
    3 tablespoons butter *or* margarine
    3 tablespoons all-purpose flour
    ¾ cup chicken broth
    ¾ cup milk
    1 cup shredded Swiss cheese
    ½ teaspoon paprika

Thaw fish if frozen (see tip, page 18). Cut and piece fillets together to make eight portions. Sprinkle with salt. Set aside.

In a 4-cup glass measure or bowl micro-cook onion in 1 tablespoon butter till onion is tender, about 1½ minutes. Stir in the salmon, parsley, and pepper. Spread about *3 tablespoons* of the filling over *each* fillet. Roll up fillets. Place, seam side down, in 10x6x2-inch baking dish; set aside. In 4-cup glass measure micro-melt the 3 tablespoons butter about 45 seconds. Blend in flour; stir in broth and milk. Micro-cook, uncovered, 1 minute; stir. Micro-cook till mixture thickens and bubbles, 3 to 4 minutes longer, stirring every 30 seconds. Pour sauce over fish rolls. Micro-cook, uncovered, till fish flakes easily when tested with a fork, 8 to 9 minutes, giving dish a quarter turn every 2 minutes and spooning sauce over fish each time. Sprinkle fish with cheese and paprika. Micro-cook, uncovered, to melt cheese, about 1 minute longer. Makes 8 servings.

Mexican-Style Tuna

In a 1-quart casserole micro-cook ¼ cup chopped onion in 1 tablespoon butter *or* margarine till tender, about 1½ minutes. Stir in one 10-ounce can mild enchilada sauce and one 8-ounce can red kidney beans, drained. Micro-cook, uncovered, till mixture is bubbly, about 3 minutes, stirring once.

Stir in one 6½- or 7-ounce can tuna, drained and flaked, and ½ cup shredded sharp American cheese. Micro-cook till cheese melts and mixture is hot, about 2 minutes more. Serve in bowls; top with slightly crushed corn *or* tortilla chips. Makes 3 or 4 servings.

Salmon Logs

    1 beaten egg
    2 tablespoons milk
    1 teaspoon lemon juice
    ¾ cup soft bread crumbs (1 slice)
    2 tablespoons snipped parsley
    ½ teaspoon instant minced onion
    ⅛ teaspoon salt
    1 7¾-ounce can salmon, drained,
          bones and skin removed, and
          flaked
          • • •
    1 tablespoon butter *or* margarine
    1 tablespoon all-purpose flour
    ½ cup milk
    ¼ cup shredded American cheese

RECIPE FOR **2**

In small bowl combine egg, milk, lemon juice, bread crumbs, parsley, onion, and salt. Add salmon; mix thoroughly. In glass pie plate shape mixture into two logs 4x2x1-inches. Micro-cook, covered, 3 minutes, giving dish a quarter turn every minute. Keep hot.

In a 2-cup glass measure micro-melt the butter 30 to 40 seconds. Blend in flour; stir in milk. Micro-cook, uncovered, till mixture thickens and bubbles, about 1½ to 2 minutes, stirring every 30 seconds. Stir in cheese till melted. Place logs on individual dinner plates. Spoon sauce atop. Makes 2 servings.

Try these two seafood specialties when you're fishing for a main dish or sandwich idea. *Sole Provencale* is elegantly laced with white wine, while *Yankee Codfish Rarebit* (see recipe, page 45) is heartily flavored with cheese and served over English muffin halves.

Halibut Steaks Teriyaki

    **4 fresh or frozen halibut steaks
        (1½ pounds)**
    ● ● ●
    **¼ cup teriyaki sauce
    2 tablespoons lemon juice
    1 tablespoon cooking oil
    ½ teaspoon dry mustard
    ½ teaspoon ground ginger
    ⅛ teaspoon garlic powder**

Thaw halibut steaks if frozen. Place halibut steaks in plastic bag. Combine teriyaki sauce, lemon juice, cooking oil, dry mustard, ground ginger, and garlic powder; pour over halibut steaks in bag. Close bag securely and place bag in pan or bowl. Marinate halibut in refrigerator 3 to 4 hours, turning occasionally. Remove halibut from marinade and arrange steaks in 12x7½x2-inch baking dish; pour marinade atop. Micro-cook, covered, until fish flakes easily when tested with a fork, about 6 minutes, turning steaks over after 3 minutes. Makes 4 servings.

Sole Provencale

Use 6 fresh *or* frozen sole fillets (1½ pounds). Thaw fish if frozen (see tip, page 18). Sprinkle each fillet with salt and paprika. Roll up fillets. Place, seam side down, in 10x6x2-inch baking dish; set aside.

In 4-cup glass measure or bowl micro-cook ¼ cup chopped onion and 1 clove garlic, minced, in 1 tablespoon butter *or* margarine, uncovered, till onion is tender, about 1½ minutes. Blend in 2 teaspoons cornstarch. Stir in one 8-ounce can tomato sauce; one 8-ounce can tomatoes, cut up; one 3-ounce can sliced mushrooms, drained; ½ cup dry white wine; 2 tablespoons snipped parsley; 1 vegetable *or* chicken bouillon cube, crushed; and 1 teaspoon sugar. Micro-cook, covered, till boiling, about 3 minutes, stirring twice.

Pour sauce over fish. Micro-cook, covered, till fish flakes easily, about 7 to 8 minutes, giving dish a quarter turn every 2 minutes and spooning sauce over fish each time. Serve fish and sauce over hot cooked rice. Serves 6.

Oriental Shrimp

> 1 7-ounce package frozen shelled
>   shrimp (2 cups)
> ¾ cup chicken broth
> 1 tablespoon cornstarch
> ¼ cup sliced green onion with
>   tops
> 2 tablespoons soy sauce
> ⅛ teaspoon ground ginger
> 1 6-ounce package frozen pea pods
> ½ cup sliced water chestnuts
> 1 small tomato, peeled and
>   cut in wedges
>   Hot cooked rice

In a 1½-quart casserole micro-cook frozen shrimp in ½ cup water, covered, till shrimp are done, 3½ to 4 minutes, stirring twice. Drain; set aside. In same casserole stir chicken broth into cornstarch; stir in onion, soy sauce, and ginger. Micro-cook, uncovered, till thickened and bubbly, about 3 minutes, stirring after each minute. Rinse pea pods in strainer under hottest tap water. Add pea pods to sauce with water chestnuts, shrimp, and tomato. Micro-cook, covered, till hot, about 2 minutes. Serve over rice. Serves 3 or 4.

How to Thaw Fish Fillets

If your microwave oven has the defrost setting, first place the frozen block of fillets in a shallow baking dish. Then, simply follow manufacturer's directions for thawing.

If your oven doesn't have the defrost feature, place a 16-ounce block of frozen fish in a baking dish, micro-cook 2 minutes, then let it rest 2 minutes. Micro-cook 1 minute; let rest 2 minutes. Again micro-cook 1 minute; let rest 2 minutes. Then, micro-cook about 30 seconds. (Turn fish over about halfway through the defrosting.) A few ice crystals will remain in center of block, but fish should be easy to separate. Outside of fish should not have started to cook.

Shrimp à la King

In 1-quart casserole micro-cook ¼ cup chopped green pepper and ¼ cup chopped onion in 2 tablespoons butter, covered, till vegetables are tender, 4 to 5 minutes. Blend in 3 tablespoons all-purpose flour, ½ teaspoon salt, and several dashes white pepper. Stir in 1 cup milk; blend in one 7-ounce package frozen shelled shrimp and one 3-ounce can sliced mushrooms, drained. Micro-cook, uncovered, 2 minutes; stir. Cook till thickened and bubbly, 5 to 6 minutes, stirring every 30 seconds. Stir in 2 tablespoons dry white wine; micro-cook 30 seconds longer. Serve over toast. Serves 6.

Seafood-Asparagus Casserole

> 2 1⅛-ounce packages hollandaise
>   sauce mix
> 1⅓ cups milk
> ½ cup dairy sour cream
>   Dash bottled hot pepper sauce
> 1 tablespoon butter *or* margarine
> ¾ cup soft bread crumbs (1 slice)
> ⅛ teaspoon paprika
> 2 8- or 10-ounce packages frozen
>   cut asparagus
> 1 6½- or 7-ounce can tuna,
>   drained and broken in pieces
> 1 4½ ounce can shrimp, drained
> 1 hard-cooked egg, sliced

Place hollandaise sauce mix in a 4-cup glass measure; gradually stir in milk. Micro-cook, uncovered, till mixture thickens and bubbles, about 4 minutes, stirring every 30 seconds. Blend in sour cream and bottled hot pepper sauce; set aside. In a small bowl micro-melt the butter 30 to 40 seconds. Toss with bread crumbs and paprika; set aside.

Place blocks of asparagus side by side in 10x6x2-inch baking dish. Micro-cook, covered, 6 minutes. Separate pieces with fork. Cook, covered, till tender, about 6 minutes. Drain well on paper toweling. Return asparagus, tuna, and shrimp to the 10x6x2-inch baking dish. Pour hollandaise sauce over all; mix well. Cook, uncovered, till hot, 5 to 6 minutes, giving dish two quarter turns during cooking. Arrange egg slices atop; sprinkle crumbs over all. Cook 30 seconds. Serves 6.

Turkey How-So

1 10¾-ounce can condensed golden
   mushroom soup
½ cup water
1 tablespoon soy sauce
1 teaspoon instant beef bouillon
   granules
1 teaspoon Worcestershire sauce
½ to 1 teaspoon curry powder
¼ teaspoon poppy seed
1 8-ounce can bamboo shoots,
   drained
½ cup sliced celery
1 small onion, cut in strips
1 small green pepper, cut in
   strips
1 3-ounce can sliced mushrooms,
   drained
2 cups cubed cooked turkey
1 3-ounce can chow mein noodles *or*
   3 cups hot cooked rice

In 2-quart casserole combine soup, water, soy, bouillon granules, Worcestershire sauce, curry, and poppy seed. Stir in bamboo shoots, celery, onion, green pepper, and mushrooms. Micro-cook, covered, till celery and onion are crisp-tender, about 8 minutes, stirring every 2 minutes. Stir in the turkey. Micro-cook, covered, till turkey is heated through, about 4 minutes, stirring twice. Serve over chow mein noodles or rice. Makes 6 servings.

Sweet-Sour Turkey

In 2-quart casserole micro-cook 1 cup bias-sliced celery and ½ cup chopped onion in 2 tablespoons butter, covered, till vegetables are crisp-tender, about 3 minutes. Stir in one 13¼-ounce can pineapple tidbits with syrup, 1 cup chicken broth, and ¼ cup packed brown sugar. Micro-cook, covered, till bubbly, 4 to 5 minutes. Meanwhile, blend ¼ cup soy sauce into 3 tablespoons cornstarch. Stir into casserole with 2 cups cubed cooked turkey.

Cook, covered, till sauce is thickened and bubbly, about 3 to 4 minutes, stirring after each minute. Stir in 3 tablespoons vinegar and 2 tablespoons lemon juice. Sprinkle ¼ cup toasted slivered almonds (see tip, page 36) atop. Serve over rice. Serves 4 or 5.

Turkey-Spinach-Rice Bake

A colortul poultry casserole shown on page 8—

1 10-ounce package frozen
   chopped spinach
½ cup chopped onion
½ cup Minute Rice
6 slices bacon
2 cups cubed cooked turkey
1 10¾-ounce can condensed
   cream of mushroom soup
½ cup dairy sour cream
¼ cup sliced water chestnuts
2 tablespoons chopped
   canned pimiento
1 tablespoon butter *or* margarine
1½ cups soft bread crumbs

In 1½-quart casserole combine spinach, onion, and ½ cup water. Micro-cook, covered, till mixture boils, 7½ to 8 minutes; stir to separate spinach. Stir in rice. Let stand, covered, 10 minutes, to absorb liquid. Place bacon between layers of paper toweling in 10x6x2-inch baking dish. Micro-cook till crisp, 6½ to 7 minutes, rearranging bacon once. Crumble bacon; stir into rice mixture with turkey, soup, sour cream, water chestnuts, pimiento, and ¼ teaspoon salt. Return to 10x6x2-inch baking dish. Cook, covered, till hot, about 10 minutes; turn dish twice. Melt the butter 30 to 40 seconds; mix with crumbs. Sprinkle atop casserole. Sprinkle with paprika, if desired. Cook, 1 minute. Makes 6 servings.

Easy Chicken and Onion Bake

In 12x7½x2-inch baking dish combine one 10½-ounce can condensed cream of chicken soup, 1 tablespoon snipped parsley, and ½ teaspoon poultry seasoning. Stir in 1½ cups frozen small whole onions. Use one 2½- to 3-pound cut up ready-to-cook broiler-fryer chicken—cut the large pieces in half. Place chicken, skin side down, in sauce in baking dish. Turn skin side up, coating with sauce.

Micro-cook, covered, until chicken is tender, about 25 minutes, rearranging chicken pieces and stirring sauce after 10 and 20 minutes. Stir sauce again before serving. Sprinkle the chicken pieces with paprika. Serve with hot cooked rice. Makes 4 servings.

Chicken Curry

 Saffron Rice
 ½ cup chopped onion
 1 clove garlic, minced
 1 tablespoon cooking oil
 1 2½ to 3-pound ready-to-cook
  broiler-fryer chicken, cut up
 2 tablespoons curry powder
 1 tablespoon cornstarch
 ½ teaspoon sugar
 ¼ cup milk
 1 medium tomato, chopped
  Condiments: Indian Chutney,
   kumquats, peanuts, shredded
   coconut, sliced green onion

Saffron Rice: In 1-quart casserole dissolve ⅛ teaspoon crushed thread saffron in 1½ cups hot water. Add 2 tablespoons butter and ¼ teaspoon salt. Micro-cook, covered, till boiling, 2½ to 3 minutes. Stir in 1½ cups Minute Rice. Cover; let stand while preparing chicken.

In 12x7½x2-inch baking dish micro-cook onion and garlic in oil, uncovered, till onion is tender, about 2 minutes. Cut large pieces of chicken in half. Arrange chicken, skin side up, in baking dish. Combine curry, cornstarch, sugar, and 1 teaspoon salt; stir in milk and ⅓ cup cold water. Mix in the tomato; pour over chicken in baking dish. Cook, covered, till chicken is done, about 25 to 28 minutes, turning dish three times and spooning sauce over chicken each time. Before serving, reheat Saffron Rice in casserole by micro-cooking, covered, 2 minutes. Transfer chicken and rice to heated serving containers. Spoon excess fat from sauce. Pour sauce over chicken. Serve with condiments. Serves 4.

Indian Chutney

In 1-quart casserole stir together 2 apples, peeled, cored, and chopped; ½ cup chopped onion; ½ cup raisins; ⅓ cup vinegar; ¼ cup packed brown sugar; ¼ cup water; 2 tablespoons chopped candied citron; 1 teaspoon curry powder; ½ teaspoon *each* salt and ground ginger; ⅛ teaspoon *each* ground cloves and cinnamon; and 1 small clove garlic, minced. Micro-cook, covered, 5 minutes; stir. Cook 3 minutes. Chill. Makes 1¾ cups.

Easy Chicken Bake

 1 2⅜-ounce package seasoned
  coating mix for chicken
 2 tablespoons grated Parmesan
  cheese
 2 tablespoons snipped parsley
 4 small whole chicken breasts
 ¼ cup milk

Place first three ingredients in plastic bag. Dip chicken in milk; shake in bag to coat. Place, skin side up, in 12x7½x2inch baking dish. Micro-cook, covered, 23 minutes. Uncover; cook till done, about 5 minutes. Serves 4.

Ginger Peachy Chicken

 1 2½ to 3-pound ready-to-cook
  broiler-fryer chicken, cut up
 1 16-ounce can peach halves
 2 tablespoons lemon juice
 2 tablespoons soy sauce
 ½ teaspoon ground ginger
 1 tablespoon cornstarch

Cut large pieces of chicken in half. Place chicken, skin side up, in 12x7½x2-inch baking dish. Sprinkle with salt. Drain peaches, reserving ½ cup syrup. Combine reserved syrup, lemon juice, soy sauce, and ginger. Set aside four peach halves. Mash remaining peaches; add to soy mixture. Drizzle over chicken.

Micro-cook, covered, till chicken is tender, about 20 to 25 minutes, rearranging chicken pieces and brushing with sauce after 10 and 15 minutes. Place reserved peaches in baking dish with chicken. Micro-cook, covered, just till peaches are hot, about 1 minute, brushing with sauce. Remove chicken and peaches to serving plate. Skim fat from sauce. Stir 2 tablespoons cold water into cornstarch; blend into juices in baking dish. Micro-cook, uncovered, till thickened and bubbly, about 3 minutes, stirring after each minute. Serve sauce with chicken and peaches. Serves 4.

Plan a microwave dinner with a foreign theme. ▶
Accompany this Indian-influenced main dish, *Chicken Curry*, with *Saffron Rice, Indian Chutney*, and other typical curry condiments such as peanuts, kumquats, onions, and coconut.

Micro-Cooked Rice

Quick, no-boil rice: In 1-quart casserole combine 1 cup water, 2 teaspoons butter, and ¼ teaspoon salt. Micro-cook till boiling, about 3 to 3½ minutes. Stir in 1 cup Minute Rice. Cover; let stand 5 minutes. Fluff with fork. Makes 2 cups.

Quick rice that needs boiling: In 1-quart casserole combine 1 cup Uncle Ben's Quick Rice, ¾ cup water, 2 teaspoons butter, and ¼ teaspoon salt. Micro-cook, covered, till rice is tender and water is absorbed, about 5 to 5½ minutes, stirring twice. Makes about 1⅓ cups.

Crab-Stuffed Chicken

  ½ cup chopped onion
  ½ cup chopped celery
  3 tablespoons butter *or* margarine
  1 7½-ounce can crab meat, drained, flaked, and cartilage removed
  ½ cup herb-seasoned stuffing mix
  5 tablespoons dry white wine
  6 whole small chicken breasts, skinned and boned
  1 envelope hollandaise sauce mix
  ¾ cup milk
  ½ cup shredded Swiss cheese

In bowl micro-cook onion and celery in butter, covered, about 2 minutes, stirring once. Stir in the crab, stuffing mix, and *3 tablespoons* of the wine. Pound chicken to flatten each breast to 8x6-inch rectangle. Sprinkle with salt and pepper. Divide stuffing mixture among chicken breasts. Roll up starting with short side; secure with wooden picks. Place in 12x7½x2-inch baking dish. Sprinkle with paprika, if desired. Micro-cook, covered, till done, about 10 minutes, turning dish once. Keep hot. In 2-cup glass measure blend sauce mix and milk. Micro-cook, uncovered, till boiling, about 2½ minutes, stirring every 30 seconds. Stir in remaining wine and cheese. Remove picks from chicken; serve with sauce. Serves 6.

Chicken Livers Peking

  1 tablespoon chopped onion
  1 tablespoon butter *or* margarine
  8 ounces chicken livers
  2 teaspoons cornstarch
  ¼ cup chicken broth
  1 2-ounce can chopped mushrooms
  1 tablespoon soy sauce
  ⅛ teaspoon ground ginger
  1 10-ounce package frozen Chinese-style vegetables
  1 3-ounce can chow mein noodles

In 1-quart casserole micro-cook onion in butter till tender, about 1½ minutes. Cut large livers in half; add livers to onion mixture, coating well. Stir in cornstarch; then mix in broth, undrained mushrooms, soy, and ginger. Place frozen vegetables with sauce atop liver mixture. Micro-cook, covered, 2 minutes. Stir to mix in vegetables. Cook, covered, 6 minutes, stirring every 2 minutes. Serve over noodles. Pass soy sauce, if desired. Serves 4.

Macaroni and Cheese

For four servings, double all ingredients except the milk (use only 1 cup)—

  1¼   cups hot tap water
  ½   cup elbow macaroni
  ⅛   teaspoon salt
         • • •
  2   tablespoons chopped onion
  1   tablespoon butter *or* margarine
  4   teaspoons all-purpose flour
  ⅔   cup milk
  ½   teaspoon Worcestershire sauce
  ¾   cup shredded sharp American cheese (2 ounces)

RECIPE FOR **2**

In 1-quart casserole combine water, macaroni, and salt. Micro-cook, uncovered, till macaroni is tender, 7 to 8 minutes, stirring twice. Drain. In same casserole micro-cook onion in butter till tender, about 1½ minutes. Blend in flour, ⅛ teaspoon salt, and dash pepper. Stir in milk and Worcestershire. Micro-cook, uncovered, till thickened and bubbly, 2 to 3 minutes, stirring every 30 seconds. Stir in cheese till melted. Stir in macaroni. Micro-cook, uncovered, till bubbly, 1 to 2 minutes longer, stirring once or twice. Makes 2 servings.

Mushroom-Sauced Eggs

2 cups fresh mushrooms (5 ounces)
4 teaspoons all-purpose flour
2 tablespoons butter *or* margarine
¾ cup milk
1½ teaspoons Worcestershire sauce
¾ teaspoon dry mustard
½ teaspoon paprika
¼ teaspoon salt
⅛ teaspoon pepper
Poached Eggs
2 English muffins, split and toasted

Chop mushrooms; sprinkle with flour. In a 1-quart casserole micro-cook mushrooms in butter, covered, about 3½ minutes, stirring after 2 minutes. Stir in milk, Worcestershire sauce, mustard, paprika, salt, and pepper. Micro-cook, uncovered, till thickened and bubbly, about 3 minutes, stirring every 30 seconds. Cover; set aside. Prepare Poached Eggs. Return mushroom sauce to microwave oven and micro-cook, covered, till heated through, 1 to 2 minutes. Place Poached Eggs on muffin halves. Spoon mushroom sauce over. Makes 2 servings.

Poached Eggs: In a 1½-quart casserole micro-cook 2 cups water till boiling, about 5 to 5½ minutes. Using 4 eggs, break eggs, one at a time, into a cup. With fork or wooden pick, carefully pierce yolk just to break membrane. Slide egg into water. Working quickly, repeat with remaining eggs. Micro-cook, uncovered, until white is firm, about 1½ to 2 minutes.

Individual Ham Loaves

1 beaten egg
¾ cup soft bread crumbs (1 slice)
2 tablespoons chopped onion
1 teaspoon Dijon-style mustard
8 ounces ground fully cooked ham
2 tablespoons orange marmalade

RECIPE FOR **2**

Mix egg, crumbs, onion, and mustard. Add ham; mix well. In 9-inch glass pie plate shape mixture into two loaves, about 4½x2½-inches. Micro-cook, covered, 6 minutes, turning plate every two minutes. Spread *each* loaf with *half* the marmalade. Micro-cook, uncovered, till meat is done, about 1 minute longer. Serves 2.

Peach-Glazed Spareribs

Golden-colored ribs shown on page 8—

2 pounds pork spareribs
1 8¾-ounce can peach slices, drained
¼ cup packed brown sugar
2 tablespoons catsup
2 tablespoons vinegar
1 tablespoons soy sauce·
1 small clove garlic, minced
½ teaspoon ground ginger
½ teaspoon salt
Dash pepper

RECIPE FOR **2**

Cut ribs in serving-size pieces. Arrange in 12x7½x2-inch baking dish. Micro-cook, covered, 15 minutes, rearranging ribs every 5 minutes. Drain off pan juices; rearrange ribs. Meanwhile, sieve peaches or puree in blender container. Stir in remaining ingredients. Pour peach mixture over ribs. Micro-cook, uncovered, till ribs are done, about 8 minutes, brushing sauce over meat and rearranging ribs every 2 minutes. Garnish with parsley and additional peach slices, if desired. Makes 2 servings.

Pork and Apples with Stuffing

6 pork cubed steaks (1½ pounds)
1 envelope brown gravy mix
¼ cup packed brown sugar
1 20-ounce can pie sliced apples
¼ cup chopped celery
2 tablespoons butter *or* margarine
1 teaspoon instant minced onion
1½ cups herb-seasoned stuffing mix
¼ teaspoon salt
½ cup hot water

Sprinkle pork with salt and pepper; arrange in 12x7½x2-inch baking dish. Set aside. In bowl combine gravy mix and sugar; break up lumps. Stir in undrained apples; spoon over meat.

In bowl micro-cook celery in butter, covered, till tender, about 2½ minutes. Stir in onion; let stand 2 minutes. Add stuffing mix and salt; toss with the water till moistened. Set aside. Micro-cook steaks, covered, 13 minutes, giving dish a half turn after 9 minutes. Stir sauce around meat. Sprinkle stuffing over meat. Micro-cook, covered, till pork is done, about 5 minutes longer. Makes 6 servings.

Convenience products make this fancy main dish especially easy to prepare. *Ham Rolls with Creamed Onions* starts with a frozen rice and vegetable mixture prepared right in its cooking pouch. The sauce that tops the ham rolls is another frozen product—onions in cream sauce.

Ham Rolls with Creamed Onions

Cook one 12-ounce package frozen rice with peas and mushrooms in cooking pouch according to package directions for microwave oven. Transfer contents of pouch to bowl; stir in ½ cup shredded sharp American cheese.

Using 8 slices boiled ham (8 ounces), spoon a scant ¼ *cup* rice mixture on *each* ham slice. Roll up, jelly roll fashion. Arrange ham rolls, seam side down, in 10-inch glass pie plate or 10x6x2-inch baking dish; set aside while preparing sauce.

In bowl combine one 9-ounce package frozen onions in cream sauce, ¾ cup water, and 1 tablespoon butter *or* margarine. Micro-cook, covered, till onions are tender and sauce is thickened, about 7 to 8 minutes, stirring twice. Micro-cook ham rolls, covered, till heated through, about 3 minutes. Uncover and spoon onions in cream sauce atop; micro-cook, uncovered, till hot, about 1 minute longer. Garnish with parsley. Makes 4 servings.

Ham and Broccoli Bake

- **2 10-ounce packages frozen chopped broccoli**
- **½ cup chopped onion**
- **2 tablespoons water**
- **2 10½-ounce cans condensed cream of chicken soup**
- **1 cup shredded sharp American cheese (4 ounces)**
- **½ cup milk**
- **3 cups chopped fully cooked ham**
- **2 cups Minute Rice**
- **½ teaspoon Worcestershire sauce**

In 2½-quart casserole micro-cook the frozen broccoli, onion, and water, covered, till vegetables are tender, about 11 minutes. Stir twice to break up broccoli. Blend in soup, cheese, and milk. Stir in ham, uncooked rice, and Worcestershire. Micro-cook, covered, 10 to 11 minutes, stirring twice. Let stand, covered, for 5 minutes. Stir before serving. Garnish with parsley, if desired. Serves 8.

Barbecued Ham and Pineapple

  1 3-pound canned ham
  1 20-ounce can pineapple slices
  ½ cup chili sauce
  ¼ cup sugar
  2 tablespoons lemon juice
  2 teaspoons Worcestershire sauce
  ½ teaspoon chili powder
  2 tablespoons cold water
  1 tablespoon cornstarch

Place ham, fat side down, in 12x7½x2-inch baking dish. Micro-cook, covered, 10 minutes, giving dish a half turn after 5 minutes. Meanwhile, drain pineapple, reserving syrup. Combine ¼ *cup* of the syrup, chili sauce, sugar, lemon juice, Worcestershire sauce, and chili powder. Turn ham over. Spoon sauce over ham.

Micro-cook, uncovered, till ham is hot, about 10 minutes, giving dish a half turn and brushing ham with sauce after 5 minutes. Remove ham from dish; cover with foil to keep warm.

Pour pan juices into a 2-cup glass measure. Add water to make 1¼ cups. Blend cold water into the cornstarch. Stir into juices in measuring cup. Micro-cook, uncovered, till thickened and bubbly, about 2 to 2½ minutes, stirring every 30 seconds. Set aside.

Place pineapple slices and remaining pineapple syrup in same 12x7½x2-inch baking dish. Micro-cook, covered, till pineapple is hot, about 3 minutes, turning dish once. Remove pineapple from syrup; brush with a little barbecue sauce. Place ham on platter. Arrange pineapple around ham. Spoon some sauce over ham and pass remaining. Serves 8 to 10.

Mixed Vegetable-Ham Bake
A curry-flavored meat and vegetable main dish—

In 2-quart casserole combine 2¼ cups beef broth, ¾ cup uncooked regular rice, ½ cup chopped onion, ⅓ cup chopped green pepper, ¼ cup chopped celery, and 1 teaspoon curry powder; mix well. Micro-cook, covered, 8 minutes, stirring after 4 minutes. Stir in 2 cups chopped fully cooked ham (10 ounces) and one 10-ounce package frozen mixed vegetables, partially thawed. Micro-cook, covered, 12 minutes more, stirring every 3 minutes. Transfer mixture to serving bowl. Makes 4 or 5 servings.

Golden-Sauced Franks
A family appealing main dish shown on the cover—

  2 18-ounce cans sweet potatoes
  1 15¼-ounce can pineapple chunks
  1½ pounds frankfurters,
      cut in 1-inch pieces
      ● ● ●
  ⅓ cup packed brown sugar
  2 tablespoons cornstarch
  ½ teaspoon grated orange peel
  ½ cup orange juice
  ¼ cup water
  2 tablespoons vinegar
  2 tablespoons chili sauce

Drain potatoes; cut up large pieces and set aside. Drain pineapple, reserving syrup. In 3-quart casserole combine potatoes, pineapple, and franks; set aside. In a 2-cup glass measure combine the brown sugar and cornstarch. Stir in the reserved pineapple syrup, orange peel, orange juice, water, vinegar, and chili sauce. Micro-cook, uncovered, till thickened and bubbly, about 3 minutes, stirring after each minute. Pour sauce over mixture in casserole. Micro-cook, covered, 12 minutes, stirring every 3 minutes. Makes 8 servings.

Pork and Rice à l'Orange
Use either rib or loin pork chops—

  ½ cup Minute Rice
  ½ cup orange juice
  2 tablespoons raisins
  1 tablespoon water
  2 teaspoons packed brown sugar
  ¼ teaspoon salt
  ⅛ teaspoon ground cinnamon
  2 pork chops, cut ½ inch thick
      (about 5 ounces each)
  Salt
  Pepper
  Paprika

RECIPE FOR 2

In 6½x6½x2-inch ceramic baking dish combine the rice, orange juice, raisins, water, brown sugar, ¼ teaspoon salt, and the cinnamon. Mix well. Place chops atop rice mixture; sprinkle meat with salt, pepper, and paprika. Micro-cook, covered, till chops and rice are done, about 9 to 10 minutes, giving dish a half turn after 5 minutes. Makes 2 servings.

Barbecued Pork Chops and Rice

½ cup Minute Rice
½ cup water
¼ teaspoon salt
  Dash chili powder
2 pork chops, cut ½ inch
    thick (about 5 ounces each)
2 thin onion slices
3 tablespoons bottled barbecue
    sauce
1 tablespoon water

RECIPE FOR **2**

In 6½x6½x2-inch ceramic baking dish combine rice, the ½ cup water, the salt, and chili powder. Place pork chops atop rice. Season chops with salt. Place an onion slice atop each chop. Combine barbecue sauce and the 1 tablespoon water; spoon over chops. Micro-cook, covered, till chops and rice are done, about 9 to 10 minutes, giving dish a half turn after 5 minutes. Makes 2 servings.

Curried Lamb Meatballs

1 beaten egg
2 tablespoons milk
1 cup soft bread crumbs
1 pound ground lamb
½ cup chopped onion
2 tablespoons butter *or* margarine
2 tablespoons all-purpose flour
4 teaspoons curry powder
¼ teaspoon paprika
¼ teaspoon dried oregano, crushed
1½ cups chicken broth
1 medium apple, peeled and chopped
  Hot cooked rice

Combine egg, milk, crumbs, and ½ teaspoon salt. Add lamb; mix well. Shape into 32 meatballs; arrange in 12x7½x2-inch baking dish. Micro-cook, covered, 6 minutes, rearranging twice; set aside. In 2-quart casserole micro-cook onion in butter, till tender, about 2 minutes. Blend in flour, curry powder, paprika, oregano, ¼ teaspoon salt, and dash pepper. Stir in broth. Micro-cook, uncovered, 1 minute; stir. Cook till thickened and bubbly, about 4 minutes, stirring every 30 seconds. Stir in meatballs. Cook, covered, 3 minutes. Stir in apple. Cook, covered, 2 minutes longer. Serve with rice. Makes 4 servings.

Sausage-Stuffed Acorn Squash

1 medium acorn squash (1 pound)
6 ounces bulk pork sausage
2 tablespoons chopped onion
1 tablespoon snipped parsley
1 small tomato, peeled and
    chopped (½ cup)
¼ cup sliced fresh mushrooms
1 small clove garlic, minced
½ teaspoon sugar

RECIPE FOR **2**

Pierce squash with metal skewer in several places. Place on paper plate. Micro-cook, uncovered, till done, 7 to 8 minutes, turning after 4 minutes. Let stand several minutes.

Crumble sausage in 1-quart casserole; add onion. Micro-cook, covered, till meat is cooked and onion is tender, about 5 minutes, stirring twice. Drain off excess fat. Set aside. Halve squash; remove seeds and string fibers. Scoop out squash; reserve shells. Stir squash, parsley, ¼ teaspoon salt, and dash pepper into sausage mixture. (If necessary, stir in milk till of desired moistness—2 to 3 tablespoons.) Fill shells with sausage mixture. Place in 10x6x2-inch baking dish. Micro-cook, covered, till hot, about 4 minutes. Let stand, covered, while preparing sauce.

In 1-quart casserole combine tomato, mushrooms, garlic, sugar, ¼ teaspoon salt, and dash pepper. Micro-cook, uncovered, till desired consistency, about 4 to 5 minutes, stirring twice. Reheat squash, if necessary, about 1 minute. Serve sauce over squash. Serves 2.

Lamb Stew

In 2-quart casserole coat 1 pound boneless lamb shoulder cut in ½-inch cubes with 1 envelope onion gravy mix. Micro-cook, covered, 5 minutes, stirring twice. In shaker jar combine 1 cup water; 2 tablespoons all-purpose flour; ½ teaspoon salt; ¼ teaspoon dried mint, crushed (optional); and ⅛ teaspoon garlic powder. Shake to blend. Stir into lamb. Stir in one 16-ounce can tomatoes, cut up; 3 medium carrots, sliced; and ½ cup chopped green pepper. Cook, covered, 20 minutes, stirring every 5 minutes. Stir in one 10-ounce package frozen peas. Cook, covered, 15 minutes longer, stirring after 8 minutes. Makes 4 servings.

Beef and Bean Cassoulet

A good use for leftover beef—

 1 8-ounce can tomato sauce with
   chopped onion
 ⅓ cup dry red wine
 ½ teaspoon salt
 ½ teaspoon dried basil, crushed
 1 clove garlic, minced
 1 15-ounce can great northern
   beans, drained
 1½ cups cubed cooked beef
 2 links Polish sausage (6 ounces),
   cut in ½-inch slices
 ½ cup cold water
 1 tablespoon all-purpose flour
 2 tablespoons snipped parsley

In a 3-quart casserole combine the tomato sauce, wine, salt, basil, and garlic. Micro-cook, uncovered, till mixture bubbles, about 5 minutes, stirring once. Stir in the beans, beef, and sausage. Micro-cook, covered, till meat and beans are heated through, about 5 minutes, stirring twice. Stir water into the flour; blend into bean-meat mixture. Micro-cook, uncovered, till mixture is thickened and bubbly, about 1 minute, stirring every 30 seconds. Serve in bowls. Sprinkle with parsley. Serves 6.

Baked Bean Chili

Use amount of chili powder that suits your taste—

 ½ pound ground beef
 ¼ cup chopped onion
 1 tablespoon chopped
   green pepper
 1 8-ounce can pork and beans
   in tomato sauce
 1 8-ounce can tomatoes, cut up
 2 tablespoons chili sauce
 2 tablespoons water
 1 to 1½ teaspoons chili powder

RECIPE FOR **2**

In a 2-quart casserole crumble ground beef. Add onion and green pepper. Micro-cook, covered, till meat is brown, about 3 to 4 minutes, stirring twice to break up meat. Drain off excess fat. Stir in undrained beans, tomatoes, chili sauce, water, chili powder, and ½ teaspoon salt. Micro-cook, uncovered, 10 minutes, stirring three times. Serve in bowls. Pass crackers, if desired. Makes 2 servings.

Savory Stuffed Peppers

 4 large green peppers
 1 pound ground beef
 1 12-ounce can whole kernel corn
 1 8-ounce can tomato sauce
 ¼ cup chopped onion
 ½ teaspoon Worcestershire sauce
 1 cup shredded sharp American
   cheese (4 ounces)

Halve peppers lengthwise; remove seeds and membranes. Place peppers in 12x7½x2-inch baking dish. Sprinkle insides with salt. Micro-cook, covered, 5 minutes. In bowl crumble ground beef. Drain corn. Add corn to meat with ½ *cup* of the tomato sauce, onion, Worcestershire, and ½ teaspoon salt. Micro-cook, covered, 7 to 8 minutes, stirring after 5 minutes. Spoon off excess fat. Stir in cheese. Spoon into pepper cups. Spoon remaining tomato sauce over peppers. Cook, uncovered, 7 to 8 minutes, turning dish once. Makes 8 servings.

Beef-Stuffed Onions

Peel 6 medium to large onions. Place in 2-quart casserole with 2 tablespoons water. Micro-cook, covered, till tender, about 13 minutes, rearranging onions after 6 minutes. Drain and cool. Remove centers of onions; chop and reserve ½ cup of the onion centers.

In same 2-quart casserole crumble 1 pound ground beef. Micro-cook, covered, till meat is brown, about 5 minutes, stirring several times to break up meat. Drain off excess fat. Stir in reserved ½ cup onion, ¾ teaspoon salt, and ¾ teaspoon dried basil, crushed. Stuff onion shells with *half* of the meat.

Stir one 8-ounce can tomato sauce with mushrooms into 1 tablespoon all-purpose flour; mix in 1 cup water and ½ teaspoon sugar. Blend into remaining meat in casserole. Arrange onions in mixture. Spoon a little sauce atop.

In a 1-cup glass measure micro-melt 1 tablespoon butter 30 to 40 seconds. Stir in ½ cup soft bread crumbs and 2 tablespoons grated Parmesan cheese; set aside. Micro-cook onions, covered, 8 minutes, turning dish after 4 minutes. Sprinkle onions with crumb mixture. Cook, uncovered, till hot, 4 to 6 minutes longer, turning dish once. Makes 6 servings.

Beef and Bean Patties

1 beaten egg
½ cup Minute Rice
⅓ cup water
1 teaspoon instant minced onion
¾ teaspoon garlic salt
¼ teaspoon seasoned pepper
1 pound lean ground beef
1 16-ounce can barbecue beans
2 tablespoons packed brown sugar
1 teaspoon Worcestershire sauce
    Dash bottled hot pepper sauce
½ cup shredded sharp American
    cheese (2 ounces)

In bowl combine egg, uncooked rice, water, onion, garlic salt, and seasoned pepper. Add beef; mix well. Shape into six 4-inch patties. Place in 12x7½x2-inch baking dish. Micro-cook, covered, till done, about 6 to 7 minutes, rearranging patties in dish after 4 minutes. Spoon off excess fat. Combine beans, brown sugar, Worcestershire sauce, and hot pepper sauce. Spoon over patties. Micro-cook, covered, till heated through, about 4 minutes, turning dish after 2 minutes. Top with cheese. Micro-cook, uncovered, till cheese melts, about 1 minute. Serve at once. Serves 6.

Micro-Burgers

¼ cup milk
2 teaspoons instant minced onion
1 beaten egg
¾ cup soft bread crumbs (1 slice)
½ teaspoon salt
    Dash pepper
1 pound lean ground beef
    Kitchen Bouquet
4 hamburger *or* frankfurter buns

In bowl combine milk and onion; let stand 5 minutes. Add egg, bread crumbs, salt, and pepper. Add ground beef; mix well. Shape into four 3-inch patties *or* four 6-inch logs. Arrange meat in 8x8x2-inch baking dish. Micro-cook, covered, for 3 minutes, giving dish a half turn once. Drain off all juices. Micro-cook, covered, till meat is done, 2 to 3 minutes more, turning dish once. Brush patties with Kitchen Bouquet. Serve in buns with catsup or barbecue sauce, if desired. Makes 4 servings.

Sweet-Sour Burgers

½ cup crushed gingersnaps (8)
1 8-ounce can tomato sauce
¼ cup finely chopped onion
¼ cup raisins
½ teaspoon salt
1 pound ground beef
2 tablespoons vinegar
2 tablespoons packed brown sugar
1 teaspoon prepared mustard

Set aside *2 tablespoons* of the crushed gingersnaps. Combine remaining gingersnaps, *2 tablespoons* of the tomato sauce, onion, raisins, and salt. Add meat; mix well. Shape into four 4-inch patties. Arrange in 8x8x2-inch baking dish. Micro-cook, covered, 5 minutes, giving dish a half turn after 3 minutes. Drain off excess fat. Combine the remaining tomato sauce, reserved gingersnaps, vinegar, brown sugar, mustard, 2 tablespoons water, and dash pepper. Pour over burgers. Micro-cook, covered, till done, about 4 minutes, stirring sauce and turning dish after 2 minutes. Serves 4.

Barbecue Cabbage Rolls

8 large cabbage leaves
1 beaten egg
3 tablespoons milk
½ cup soft bread crumbs
¼ cup finely chopped onion
¾ teaspoon salt
¼ teaspoon dried thyme, crushed
⅛ teaspoon pepper
1 pound ground beef
1 15½-ounce can sandwich sauce

In a 3-quart casserole combine cabbage and ½ cup water. Micro-cook, covered, till leaves are pliable, about 8 minutes. Let stand, covered, till cool. Combine egg, milk, crumbs, onion, salt, thyme, and pepper. Add meat; mix well. Place about ¼ *cup* meat in center of *each* cabbage leaf; fold in sides and roll ends over meat mixture. Place rolls, seam side down, in 12x7½x2-inch baking dish. Pour sandwich sauce over. Micro-cook, covered, till meat is done and cabbage is tender, about 14 minutes, giving dish a quarter turn every 4 minutes. Remove cabbage rolls to serving plate. Stir sauce in dish; serve with rolls. Serves 4.

Tangy Meat Loaf

    1 beaten egg
    1 cup dairy sour cream
    ½ cup coarsely crushed saltine
        crackers (11 crackers)
    ½ cup shredded carrot
    1¼ teaspoons salt
    ⅛ teaspoon pepper
        • • •
    1 pound ground beef
    ½ pound ground pork

In bowl combine beaten egg, dairy sour cream, cracker crumbs, shredded carrot, salt, and pepper; mix well. Add ground beef and pork; combine thoroughly. In a 9-inch glass pie plate shape meat mixture into a ring about 1 inch high around a small juice glass having a 2-inch diameter. Micro-cook, covered, till meat is done, about 13 minutes, giving dish a quarter turn every 3 minutes. Remove the glass. Let meat stand 5 minutes before removing to serving plate. If desired, brush meat loaf with Kitchen Bouquet. Makes 6 servings.

Everyday Meat Loaf

    2 beaten eggs
    ¾ cup milk
    ½ cup fine dry bread crumbs
    ¼ cup finely chopped onion
    2 tablespoons snipped parsley
    1 teaspoon salt
    ¾ teaspoon ground sage
    ⅛ teaspoon pepper
    1½ pounds ground beef

In bowl combine beaten eggs, milk, fine dry bread crumbs, onion, parsley, salt, sage, and pepper; mix well. Add ground beef; combine thoroughly. In a 9-inch glass pie plate shape meat mixture into a ring about 1 inch high around a small juice glass having a 2-inch diameter. Micro-cook, covered, till meat is done, about 12 to 13 minutes, giving dish a quarter turn every 3 minutes. Remove the juice glass. Let meat loaf stand 5 minutes before removing to serving plate. If desired, garnish with tomato wedges and parsley; or, serve meat loaf with warmed catsup; or, sprinkle with shredded American cheese before letting meat stand for the 5 minutes. Makes 6 servings.

Oriental Beef Ring

A favorite main dish shown on page 8—

    1 3-ounce can chow mein noodles
    1 8-ounce can tomato sauce with
        chopped onion
    1 beaten egg
    ¼ cup chopped celery
    2 tablespoons soy sauce
    ⅛ teaspoon ground ginger
    1 pound ground beef
    1 tablespoon packed brown sugar
    2 teaspoons soy sauce
    1 6-ounce package frozen pea pods
    1 tablespoon butter *or* margarine

Finely crush *1 cup* of the noodles; combine with ⅔ *cup* of the tomato sauce. Let stand 5 minutes to soften. In large bowl combine egg, celery, the 2 tablespoons soy sauce, ginger, and noodle mixture. Add beef; mix well. Press into an oiled 3-cup ring mold (6½ inches in diameter and 2½ inches deep). Loosen edges. Invert mold into a 9-inch glass pie plate; *remove mold.* Micro-cook, covered with waxed paper, till done, about 10 minutes, turning dish every 3 minutes. Drain off excess fat. Combine remaining tomato sauce, sugar, and 2 teaspoons soy sauce; brush on meat ring. Cook, uncovered, 30 seconds. Cover; keep hot.

In a 1-quart casserole combine pea pods and 2 tablespoons water. Micro-cook, covered, till tender, about 4 minutes, tossing twice with a fork. Drain. Toss with remaining chow mein noodles and butter. Micro-cook, uncovered, 15 seconds. Transfer meat to serving plate. Surround with vegetable mixture. Serves 6.

Meat Loaf Toppers

To dress up a meat loaf try some of these simple suggestions: Spread chili sauce, barbecue sauce, pizza sauce, or enchilada sauce over the top of the meat after removing from the microwave oven. Or, sprinkle with Parmesan cheese or arrange cheese wedges over the top of the hot meat loaf and let the cheese melt.

Blend versatile ground beef with a cheese sauce and frozen vegetables and what do you have? *Cheeseburger-Vegetable Casserole!* Dress up the mashed potato topper with a sprinkling of cheese. Then, round out the meal with relishes, rolls, dessert, and a beverage.

Cheeseburger-Vegetable Casserole

    1 pound ground beef
    ½ cup chopped onion
            • • •
    ¼ cup butter *or* margarine
    ¼ cup all-purpose flour
    1 teaspoon salt
      Dash pepper
  1½ cups milk
  1½ cups shredded sharp American
        cheese (6 ounces)
    1 teaspoon Worcestershire sauce
    1 10-ounce package frozen
        mixed vegetables
    ¼ cup chopped canned pimiento
      Packaged instant mashed
        potatoes (enough for 4
        servings)

In a large bowl crumble the ground beef. Add the chopped onion. Micro-cook, covered, till meat is brown, about 5 minutes, stirring several times to break up meat. Drain off excess fat. In a 4-cup glass measure micro-melt the butter about 45 seconds. Stir in the flour, salt, and pepper. Gradually stir in the milk. Micro-cook, uncovered, 1 minute; stir. Micro-cook till thickened and bubbly, about 3 minutes more, stirring every 30 seconds. Stir in *1 cup* of the cheese and the Worcestershire sauce. Add to meat mixture. Break up frozen vegetables. Stir vegetables and pimiento into meat mixture. Turn mixture into an 8x8x2-inch baking dish. Micro-cook, covered, 10 minutes, turning after 5 minutes.

Prepare the packaged instant mashed potatoes according to package directions *except* decrease water by ¼ cup. Spoon the prepared potatoes around edge of casserole. Sprinkle remaining shredded American cheese over potatoes. Micro-cook, uncovered, till cheese is melted, about 1 minute. Serves 4 to 6.

Mexican-Style Lasagna

    1 pound ground beef
    ½ cup chopped onion
    1 16-ounce can tomatoes, cut up
    1 10½-ounce can pizza sauce
    ¼ cup sliced pitted ripe olives
    ½ teaspoon salt
    ¼ teaspoon dried oregano, crushed
    1 beaten egg
    1 cup shredded American cheese
    1 cup cream-style cottage cheese
    4 cups corn-flavor tortilla chips
        (4 ounces)

In 12x7½x2-inch baking dish crumble ground beef. Add onion; micro-cook, covered, till meat is brown, about 5 minutes, stirring several times to break up meat. Drain off excess fat. Stir in tomatoes, pizza sauce, olives, salt, oregano, and dash pepper. Micro-cook, covered, 8 minutes; stir once. Transfer to another dish.

In a bowl combine egg and cheeses. Set aside *eight* of the tortilla chips; slightly crush remaining chips. Spread *one-third* of the meat mixture in the 12x7½x2-inch baking dish; top with *half* of the cheese mixture, and *half* of the crushed tortilla chips. Repeat layers, ending with meat. Micro-cook, uncovered, 10 minutes, turning dish twice. Top with reserved chips. Let stand 5 minutes. Makes 6 servings.

Ravioli Casserole

    ¼ cup cold water
    1 tablespoon all-purpose flour
    1 cup beef broth
    2 15-ounce cans beef ravioli
        in sauce
    1½ to 2 cups cubed cooked beef
    1 16-ounce can cut green beans,
        drained
    1 3-ounce can chopped
        mushrooms, drained
    ¼ cup grated Parmesan cheese

In 2-quart casserole stir water into flour; stir in broth. Micro-cook, uncovered, till thickened and bubbly, about 5 minutes, stirring after each minute. Stir in the ravioli in sauce, beef, beans, and mushrooms. Micro-cook, covered, till hot, 7 to 8 minutes, stirring four times. Sprinkle cheese atop. Serves 6.

Milwaukee Mix-Up

In 2-quart casserole combine 2 medium potatoes, peeled and sliced; ½ cup water; and ¾ teaspoon salt. Micro-cook, covered, till potatoes are tender, about 7 minutes, giving dish a quarter turn every 2 minutes. Drain; set aside.

In same casserole crumble 1 pound ground beef. Add ½ cup chopped onion, ¼ cup chopped green pepper, and ½ teaspoon salt. Micro-cook, covered, till meat is brown and vegetables are tender, about 5 minutes, stirring several times to break up meat. Drain off excess fat. Stir in 2 tablespoons all-purpose flour, 1 teaspoon instant beef bouillon granules, 1 teaspoon sugar, and ½ teaspoon caraway seed. Stir in 1 cup water. Cook, covered, till thickened and bubbly, about 4 minutes, stirring after each minute. Stir in one 16-ounce can sauerkraut, drained and snipped, and 2 tablespoons chopped canned pimiento. Carefully stir in potatoes. Cook, covered, till hot, about 5 minutes, carefully stirring three times. Sprinkle ½ cup shredded Swiss cheese over top. Cook, uncovered, to melt cheese, about 30 seconds. Serve with dairy sour cream. Serves 4.

Sour Cream-Chili Bake

    1 pound ground beef
    ¼ cup chopped onion
    1 10-ounce can hot enchilada
        sauce
    1 8-ounce can tomato sauce
    1 15-ounce can pinto beans
    2⅓ cups crushed corn chips
    1 cup shredded sharp American
        cheese (4 ounces)
    1 cup dairy sour cream

In 2-quart casserole crumble ground beef. Add onion; micro-cook, covered, till meat is brown, about 5 minutes, stirring several times to break up meat. Drain off excess fat. Stir in enchilada sauce and tomato sauce. Micro-cook, covered, 5 minutes, stirring once. Drain beans; stir beans, *1 cup* of the corn chips, and ¾ *cup* of the cheese into meat. Micro-cook, covered, 6 minutes, stirring once. Stir, then spread sour cream over top; sprinkle remaining chips and cheese over top. Cook just till sour cream is hot, 30 to 45 seconds. Serves 6 to 8.

A Variety of Vegetables

*M*icrowave cooking is an excellent way to prepare colorful, flavorful, and nutritious vegetables, as you'll see on the next few pages. When preparing vegetables, cook them just till they are almost done. (They will finish cooking with the stored heat in the cooked vegetables.)

Orange-Sauced Carrots

    6 to 8 carrots, sliced ⅛ inch
        thick (3 cups)
    ⅓ cup water
    1 tablespoon packed brown sugar
    1½ teaspoons cornstarch
    ⅔ cup orange juice
    1 tablespoon butter *or* margarine
    ¼ teaspoon salt
    ⅛ teaspoon ground ginger
        Dash ground cloves

In a 1-quart casserole place sliced carrots and water. Micro-cook carrots, covered, till tender, 9 to 10 minutes. Drain well.

Stir together brown sugar and cornstarch; blend in orange juice, butter, salt, ginger, and cloves. Stir mixture into carrots. Micro-cook, uncovered, 2 minutes; stir. Cook, uncovered, 1 to 1½ minutes longer. Serves 4.

German-Style Spinach

    1 slice bacon
    1 tablespoon chopped onion
    2 teaspoons vinegar
    1 teaspoon sugar
    1 7¾-ounce can leaf
        spinach, drained

RECIPE FOR **2**

Place bacon in a 1-quart casserole; cover with paper toweling. Micro-cook till crisp, about 1½ minutes. Remove bacon; drain. Reserve drippings in casserole. Crumble bacon; set aside. In reserved drippings cook onion till tender, about 1½ minutes. Stir in vinegar and sugar; stir in spinach. Micro-cook, covered, till heated through, 2 to 2½ minutes. Sprinkle with crumbled bacon. Makes 2 servings.

Spinach Elegante

    1 10-ounce package frozen
        Welsh rarebit
    8 slices bacon
    2 10-ounce packages frozen
        chopped spinach
    ½ of an 8-ounce can water
        chestnuts, drained and
        sliced (½ cup)
    ½ of a 3½-ounce can French-fried
        onions (about ¾ cup)

Remove frozen rarebit from foil pan; place in a 1-quart casserole. Micro-cook, covered, 5 minutes, stirring once. Set aside. In a 10x6x2-inch baking dish place bacon between layers of paper toweling, layering bacon and toweling, if needed. Cook about 7 minutes, rearranging once. Remove bacon and toweling; crumble bacon. Set aside. Drain off excess drippings.

Place spinach in same baking dish. Cook, covered, 6 minutes, stirring once. Drain. Season with salt. Stir in water chestnuts and ⅓ cup of the rarebit. Sprinkle with bacon.

Spread remaining rarebit over all. Top with onion rings. Micro-cook, uncovered, till hot, about 5 minutes, turning dish once. Serves 6.

Oriental Peas

In a 1-quart casserole place one 6- *or* 7-ounce package frozen pea pods; ½ of an 8-ounce can water chestnuts, drained and sliced (½ cup); and 1 tablespoon chopped canned pimiento. Pour 1 tablespoon water and 1 tablespoon soy sauce over all. Micro-cook, covered, 2 minutes; stir with fork to break apart pea pods. Cook, covered, 2 minutes more; stir well. Cook, covered, till vegetables are heated through, about 1 minute longer. Makes 4 servings.

Crisp-fried onions adorn colorful *Spinach Elegante*. Smothered with a rich Welsh rarebit, this tantalizing casserole is made with chopped spinach, water chestnuts, and crumbled bacon. ▸

Basil Beans

8 ounces fresh green beans,
 cut in pieces (2 cups)
2 tablespoons chopped onion
2 tablespoons chopped celery
2 tablespoons butter *or* margarine
½ teaspoon dried basil, crushed
¼ teaspoon salt
 Dash pepper

RECIPE FOR 2

In a 1-quart casserole micro-cook beans, onion, celery, and ¼ cup water, covered, till beans are almost tender, about 9 minutes, stirring after 5 minutes. *Do not drain*. Stir in remaining ingredients. Micro-cook, covered, till butter melts, about 1 minute. Serves 2 or 3.

Hominy-Bean Bake

1 16-ounce can yellow
 hominy, drained
1 15½-ounce can cut green
 beans, drained
1 cup meatless spaghetti sauce
 or Italian cooking sauce
2 tablespoons finely
 chopped celery
1 teaspoon sugar
½ teaspoon Worcestershire sauce
½ cup coarsely crushed corn chips

In a 1½-quart casserole combine all ingredients *except* corn chips. Micro-cook, covered, till heated through, 8 to 9 minutes, stirring every 3 minutes. Top with corn chips. Serves 6.

Easy Baked Beans

Place 4 slices bacon in a 1½-quart casserole; cover with paper toweling. Micro-cook till crisp, 3½ to 4 minutes. Remove bacon; drain. Reserve about 3 tablespoons drippings in casserole. Crumble bacon and set aside.

Micro-cook ½ cup chopped onion in reserved drippings till tender, 2 minutes. Stir in two 16-ounce cans pork and beans in tomato sauce, 2 tablespoons packed brown sugar, 2 tablespoons catsup, 1 tablespoon Worcestershire sauce, and 1 tablespoon prepared mustard. Cook, uncovered, till bubbly, about 10 minutes; stir twice. Top with bacon. Serves 6.

Cheese-Sauced Brussels Sprouts

Garnish with chopped egg for a colorful effect—

2 8- or 10-ounce packages frozen
 Brussels sprouts
¼ cup water
2 tablespoons butter *or* margarine
2 tablespoons all-purpose flour
⅛ teaspoon salt
¾ cup milk
1 cup shredded sharp American
 cheese (4 ounces)
1 hard-cooked egg, chopped

In a 1½-quart casserole place Brussels sprouts and water. Micro-cook, covered, till tender, 11 to 12 minutes, stirring every 4 minutes. Drain; halve sprouts. Return to casserole.

In a 2-cup glass measure micro-melt the butter 30 to 40 seconds. Blend in flour and salt; add milk all at once, stirring well. Micro-cook, uncovered, 1 minute; stir. Micro-cook till thickened and bubbly, 2 to 3 minutes, stirring every 30 seconds. Add cheese; stir till melted. Pour over Brussels sprouts. Micro-cook, covered, till heated through, about 1 minute more; stir. Sprinkle chopped egg atop casserole. Makes 6 servings.

Corn-Stuffed Onions

Drape this vegetable dish with a cheese sauce—

6 medium onions
1 12-ounce can whole kernel corn
 with sweet peppers, drained
2 tablespoons butter *or* margarine
1 10½-ounce can condensed cream
 of celery soup
1 cup shredded sharp American
 cheese (4 ounces)

Peel and hollow out onions; chop centers to make 1 cup. Fill onion shells with corn; reserve remaining corn. Place stuffed onions in 8x8x2-inch baking dish. Micro-cook, covered, 12 minutes, turning dish once; set aside.

In a 4-cup glass measure or bowl micro-cook chopped onion in butter till tender, 2 to 3 minutes. Stir in soup, cheese, and remaining corn. Micro-cook, uncovered, 1 minute; stir till cheese is melted. Spoon sauce over onions. Micro-cook, uncovered, till heated through, about 4 minutes. Makes 6 servings.

Zucchini with Corn

1 tablespoon butter *or* margarine
1 small zucchini, sliced
2 tablespoons sliced green
   onion with tops
1 8¾-ounce can whole kernel
   corn, drained
Salt and pepper

RECIPE FOR **2**

In 1-quart casserole micro-melt the butter 30 to 40 seconds. Stir in zucchini and onion. Micro-cook, covered, 3 minutes. Stir in corn. Cook, covered, till zucchini is almost done and corn is hot, about 3 minutes. Season to taste with salt and pepper. Makes 2 or 3 servings.

Dilled Zucchini

In a 1½-quart casserole combine 6 cups sliced zucchini (about 1½ pounds); ¼ cup water; and ½ teaspoon salt. Micro-cook, covered, till almost done, 12 to 13 minutes, stirring twice. Keep hot while preparing dill sauce.

In a 2-cup glass measure micro-melt 2 tablespoons butter *or* margarine for 30 to 40 seconds. Blend in 1 tablespoon all-purpose flour, 1 teaspoon lemon juice, ½ teaspoon salt, ½ teaspoon paprika, and ½ teaspoon dried dill-weed. Stir in ½ cup milk. Micro-cook sauce, uncovered, for 1 minute; stir. Cook till sauce is thickened and bubbly, about 1½ minutes more, stirring every 30 seconds.

Drain cooked zucchini. Pour dill sauce over vegetable and mix thoroughly. If necessary, micro-cook just till hot. Makes 6 servings.

Harvard Beets

1 8¼-ounce can sliced beets
1 tablespoon sugar
1 teaspoon cornstarch
2 tablespoons vinegar
1 tablespoon butter *or* margarine

RECIPE FOR **2**

Drain beets; reserve ¼ cup of the liquid. In a 2-cup glass measure mix sugar, cornstarch, and ⅛ teaspoon salt. Stir in reserved liquid, vinegar, and butter. Micro-cook, uncovered, till thickened and bubbly, 1 minute; stir every 15 seconds. Stir in beets. Cook, covered, till hot, about 2 minutes. Serves 2.

Drying Fresh Herbs

Enjoy your garden-fresh herbs all year long by drying a few favorites in the microwave oven. Wash 1 cup fresh mint leaves *or* parsley sprigs thoroughly; shake off excess water. (Measure herbs by packing loosely in cup.) Arrange mint or parsley in a single layer on a double thickness of paper toweling. Place a single layer of paper toweling on top. Micro-cook until herbs are *thoroughly* dried and can be crumbled, about 3 to 4 minutes. Store in tightly covered containers. Makes about ⅓ cup dried herb.

Try your hand at drying other fresh herbs, following the basic directions given above.

Wilted Leaf Lettuce
Serve greens warm, yet slightly crisp—

6 slices bacon
½ cup sliced green onion
¼ cup vinegar
¼ cup water
1 tablespoon sugar
½ teaspoon salt

• • •

4 cups torn leaf lettuce
4 cups torn fresh spinach
6 radishes, thinly sliced
2 hard-cooked eggs, chopped

Place bacon slices in a large glass bowl; cover with paper toweling. Micro-cook till bacon is crisp, 4 to 5 minutes. Remove bacon and drain thoroughly, reserving ¼ cup drippings in bowl. Crumble bacon and set aside.

Micro-cook onion in reserved drippings in bowl for 3 minutes. Add vinegar, water, sugar, and salt. Cook, uncovered, till boiling, about 1½ minutes. Stir to dissolve sugar. Place lettuce and spinach in same bowl; toss to coat well with dressing. Micro-cook, uncovered, 1 minute, tossing salad after 30 seconds.

Serve in salad bowl garnished with crumbled bacon, radishes, and eggs. Makes 6 servings.

Scalloped Succotash

¼ cup chopped onion
2 17-ounce cans whole kernel corn
1 17-ounce can lima beans, drained
1 10½-ounce can condensed
  cream of celery soup
1½ cups coarsely crushed saltine
  crackers (33 crackers)
½ cup shredded Swiss cheese
¼ cup milk
¼ cup chopped canned pimiento
  Dash pepper
1 tablespoon butter *or* margarine

In 2½-quart casserole micro-cook onion in 2 tablespoons water, covered, till onion is tender, 1½ minutes; drain. Drain corn, reserving ¾ cup of the liquid. In same casserole mix onion, reserved corn liquid, corn, lima beans, soup, *1¼ cups* of the crumbs, Swiss cheese, milk, pimiento, and pepper.

In small bowl micro-melt the butter 30 to 40 seconds; toss with remaining ¼ cup crumbs. Set aside. Micro-cook casserole, uncovered, 18 minutes, stirring every 5 minutes. Let stand 2 to 3 minutes before serving. Sprinkle with reserved buttered crumbs; garnish with parsley and cherry tomatoes, if desired. Makes 12 servings.

Creamy Vegetable Bake

Peel 1 pound carrots (about 8 carrots); quarter lengthwise and cut in 2-inch pieces. In 2-quart glass bowl or casserole combine carrots; 2 cups frozen Southern-style hashed brown potatoes (8 ounces); ¾ cup sliced celery; ½ cup chopped onion; one 3-ounce can sliced mushrooms, drained; ¼ cup water; and ½ teaspoon salt. Micro-cook, covered, till tender, about 18 minutes, stirring every 5 minutes. *Do not drain.* Sprinkle 1 envelope white sauce mix (enough for 1 cup sauce) over vegetables; blend gently. Gradually stir in 2 cups milk. Cook, covered, till thickened and bubbly, about 5 minutes, stirring after each minute.

Gently stir in ½ cup dairy sour cream. Turn into 1½-quart casserole. Cook, covered, till hot, about 3 minutes. Circle edge of casserole with *half* of a 3½-ounce can French-fried onions (about 1 cup); cook, uncovered, 30 seconds. Trim with parsley. Makes 6 servings.

Golden Crumb Bean Casserole

2 9-ounce packages frozen whole
  or cut green beans
⅓ cup water
1 10¾-ounce can condensed
  cream of mushroom soup
¼ cup mayonnaise *or* salad dressing
2 tablespoons chopped
  canned pimiento
1 teaspoon lemon juice
⅓ cup finely crushed round cheese
  crackers (8 crackers)

In 1½-quart casserole micro-cook beans in the water, covered, 12 minutes; stir every 3 minutes. Drain; set beans aside. In same dish mix soup and next 3 ingredients; stir in beans. Cook, covered, 2 minutes. Stir; cook, covered, till hot, 2 minutes. Sprinkle with crumbs; cook, uncovered, 1 minute. Serves 6.

Onions in Cream Sauce

Peel 2 pounds small onions. In 1½-quart casserole micro-cook onions in 2 tablespoons water, covered, till tender, 10 minutes. Drain; set onions aside. In same dish micro-melt 2 tablespoons butter 30 to 40 seconds. Blend in 2 tablespoons all-purpose flour. Stir in 1 cup milk; 1 teaspoon instant chicken bouillon granules; 1 teaspoon Worcestershire sauce; ¼ teaspoon dried marjoram, crushed; and dash pepper. Cook, uncovered, 1 minute; stir. Cook till thickened and bubbly, 3 minutes; stir every 30 seconds. Stir in onions. Cook, covered, till hot, 3 minutes, stirring once. Blend ¼ cup of the sauce into ½ cup dairy sour cream; stir into onions. Top with 2 tablespoons toasted slivered almonds (see tip below). Dash with paprika. Makes 5 or 6 servings.

How to Toast Nuts

Spread about ¼ cup nuts on a paper plate or in a glass pie plate. Micro-cook, uncovered, till toasted, about 3 minutes, stirring frequently.

Try these flavorsome vegetable casseroles. Both of the mouth-watering casseroles sport an appealing topping—French-fried onions on the *Creamy Vegetable Bake* and cracker crumbs on the *Scalloped Succotash*. And each one is made with a quick-cooking sauce.

Onion-Cauliflower Bake

    1 10-ounce package frozen cauliflower
    1 10-ounce package frozen onions in cream sauce
    ⅓ cup water
    ½ cup shredded American cheese (2 ounces)
    1 tablespoon snipped parsley

In 1½-quart casserole micro-defrost frozen cauliflower, covered, about 4 minutes, breaking apart cauliflower block with a fork twice. Cut up large cauliflower pieces; return all to casserole. Add frozen onions in cream sauce and water to cauliflower. Micro-cook, covered, till done, 8 to 9 minutes, stirring three times. Stir in cheese; micro-cook, covered, for 2 to 3 minutes, stirring twice to melt cheese. Garnish with parsley. Makes 6 servings.

Elegant Stuffed Potatoes

Scrub 4 medium baking potatoes; prick several times with a fork. In microwave oven arrange potatoes on paper toweling, leaving at least 1 inch between potatoes. Micro-cook till done, 13 to 15 minutes; rearrange after 8 minutes. When done, halve lengthwise. Scoop out inside; reserve shells. In small mixing bowl combine potatoes, ½ cup cream-style cottage cheese with chives, ¼ cup butter *or* margarine, 1 teaspoon seasoned salt, and dash pepper. Beat to fluffy consistency, adding about ¼ cup milk. If desired, fold in one 2-ounce can chopped mushrooms, drained. Pile into reserved shells. Arrange on serving plate.

Micro-cook, uncovered, 4 minutes; give dish half turn after 2 minutes. Top with ½ cup shredded American cheese. Cook, uncovered, till melted, 30 to 45 seconds. Serves 8.

COOKING FROZEN VEGETABLES

Unwrap one 9- or 10-ounce package of frozen vegetables *or* measure 1½ cups loose-pack vegetables. Place in a 1-quart casserole. Follow any special instructions below. Cover. Micro-cook following times suggested, stirring, breaking up, or redistributing vegetables after half of cooking. Timings are approximate because of the wide variety of appliances available and because vegetables vary in freshness. Be sure to test them for doneness after the shorter cooking time; if necessary, continue cooking till vegetables are almost done. They will finish cooking with stored heat. *Do not overcook vegetables.* Season with salt after cooking; butter, if desired.

VEGETABLE	SPECIAL INSTRUCTIONS	APPROXIMATE TIME
Asparagus	Add 2 tablespoons water	6 to 8 minutes
Beans, Green	Add 2 tablespoons water	6 to 8 minutes
Beans, Lima	Add ½ cup water	8 to 10 minutes
Broccoli	Add 2 tablespoons water	6 to 8 minutes
Brussels Sprouts	Add 2 tablespoons water	7 to 9 minutes
Carrots	Add 2 tablespoons water	7 to 8 minutes
Cauliflower	Add 2 tablespoons water	6 to 8 minutes
Corn, Cut	Add 2 tablespoons water	4 to 6 minutes
Mixed Vegetables	Add 2 tablespoons water	5 to 7 minutes
Peas	Add 2 tablespoons water	4 to 6 minutes
Spinach	Add no water	5 to 7 minutes

Corn on the Cob

Husk and silk corn. Wrap each ear in waxed paper; twist ends of paper. Arrange corn on paper toweling; allow at least 1 inch between ears. Micro-cook one ear about 2 minutes; two ears 3 to 4 minutes; four ears 6 to 7 minutes; and six ears 8 to 10 minutes. Halfway through cooking, rearrange corn and turn over.

Or, omit wrapping in waxed paper; place husked and silked corn in baking dish. Micro-cook, covered, following times given above. Halfway through cooking time, rearrange corn.

Baked Potatoes

Select baking potatoes of approximately the same size and shape (about 8 ounces each.) Scrub potatoes and prick skin with a fork.

In microwave oven arrange potatoes on paper toweling, leaving at least 1 inch between potatoes. Micro-cook, uncovered, till potatoes test done when pricked with a fork. Allow 6 to 8 minutes for two potatoes; 13 to 15 minutes for four potatoes; and 17 to 19 minutes for six potatoes. Halfway through cooking time, rearrange potatoes and turn over.

Herbed Potatoes

8 small new potatoes
3 tablespoons butter *or* margarine
2 tablespoons finely
   snipped parsley
1 tablespoon finely snipped chives
1 teaspoon lemon juice
¼ teaspoon dried dillweed
⅛ teaspoon salt
   Dash pepper

Scrub potatoes with a coarse brush; prick several times with a fork. Place paper toweling in bottom of 10x6x2-inch baking dish. Arrange potatoes atop toweling, about 1 inch apart. Micro-cook potatoes, uncovered, till tender, 8 to 9 minutes; give dish a quarter turn every 3 minutes. Remove toweling; add butter to dish with potatoes. Micro-melt the butter about 30 to 45 seconds. Add parsley and remaining ingredients; stir potatoes to coat. Turn into serving bowl. Makes 4 servings.

Scalloped Potatoes

3 medium potatoes, peeled and
   thinly sliced (1 pound)
½ cup chopped onion
½ cup water
¼ cup chopped green pepper
1 tablespoon butter *or* margarine
1 tablespoon all-purpose flour
1 cup milk
½ teaspoon Worcestershire sauce
1 tablespoon butter *or* margarine
3 tablespoons fine dry
   bread crumbs

In 1½-quart casserole mix first four ingredients. Micro-cook, covered, 9 to 10 minutes; stir every 3 minutes. Drain; set aside. In a 2-cup glass measure micro-melt 1 tablespoon butter 30 to 40 seconds. Stir in flour, ¾ teaspoon salt, and dash pepper. Add milk and Worcestershire. Micro-cook, uncovered, 1 minute; stir. Cook till thickened and bubbly, about 1½ minutes; stir every 30 seconds. Pour over potatoes in casserole. Cook, uncovered, 2 minutes; stir after 1 minute. Season to taste. In a 1-cup glass measure micro-melt remaining butter 30 to 40 seconds. Stir in crumbs. Sprinkle over potatoes. Makes 6 servings.

Hot Potato Salad

3 medium potatoes, peeled and
   thinly sliced (1 pound)
½ cup water
4 slices bacon, chopped
½ cup chopped onion
2 tablespoons all-purpose flour
½ cup vinegar
3 tablespoons sugar
1 teaspoon salt
   Dash pepper
2 tablespoons snipped parsley

In 1½-quart casserole combine potatoes and water. Micro-cook, covered, 9 to 10 minutes; stir every 3 minutes. Drain; remove potatoes from casserole. In same casserole cook bacon and onion, covered with paper toweling, 3½ minutes; stir after 2 minutes. Stir in flour. Blend in vinegar, sugar, salt, pepper, and ⅓ cup water. Micro-cook uncovered, till bubbly, about 1½ minutes; stir every 30 seconds. Add potatoes. Cook, covered, till heated through, about 2 minutes; stir after 1 minute. Stir in parsley. Makes 4 to 6 servings.

Sweet Potato-Apple Bake

3 medium sweet potatoes
2 tart apples, peeled and
   thinly sliced (2 cups)
2 tablespoons butter *or* margarine
   Maple-flavored syrup
½ teaspoon ground cinnamon
2 tablespoons snipped parsley

Select potatoes of same size (7 to 8 ounces each). Scrub and prick skin. In microwave oven arrange potatoes on paper toweling leaving at least 1-inch between potatoes. Micro-cook till done, 10 to 12 minutes; halfway through, rearrange potatoes and turn over. When cool enough to handle, peel; slice about ⅓ inch thick (3 cups). In 1½-quart casserole toss potatoes with apples.

In a 1-cup glass measure micro-melt the butter 30 to 40 seconds; add syrup to make ⅓ cup. Stir in cinnamon and ½ teaspoon salt; pour over potato mixture in casserole. Stir gently to coat. Micro-cook, covered, till apples are tender, 5 to 6 minutes; stir gently three times. Sprinkle with parsley. Makes 6 to 8 servings.

Savory Soups and Sauces

When time is short, use your microwave oven for preparing quick-cooking soups and sauces. This section offers a selection of easy-to-assemble soups that require only a few minutes cooking in the microwave oven, and you'll find a host of tantalizing quick-cooking sauces.

Quick Fish Chowder

  1 16-ounce package frozen
     fish fillets
  2 cups frozen hashed brown potatoes
     with onion and peppers
     (8 ounces)
  ½ cup water
  ½ cup chopped onion
     ● ● ●
  1 10½-ounce can condensed
     cream of shrimp soup
  2¾ cups milk
  ¼ cup snipped parsley
  1 teaspoon salt
  ½ teaspoon dried thyme, crushed
  2 tablespoons all-purpose flour
     Paprika
     Butter *or* margarine

Thaw frozen fish fillets (see tip, page 18). Cut fish into bite-size pieces; set aside.

In a 2-quart casserole combine frozen hashed brown potatoes, water, and chopped onion. Micro-cook, covered, till vegetables are tender, 6 to 7 minutes. Do not drain.

Blend condensed cream of shrimp soup into vegetable mixture; stir in fish pieces, *2 cups* of the milk, snipped parsley, salt, and crushed thyme. Micro-cook, covered, till fish flakes easily with a fork, 6 to 8 minutes.

Stir remaining ¾ cup milk into flour; stir into fish mixture. Micro-cook, uncovered, till slightly thickened and bubbly, 6 to 8 minutes, stirring every 2 minutes. Let stand 2 to 3 minutes before serving.

To serve, sprinkle each serving with a dash of paprika and dot with a little butter or margarine. Makes 6 to 8 servings.

Seafood-Corn Chowder

  3 slices bacon, chopped
  1 7½-ounce can minced clams
  ½ cup chopped onion
     Dash bottled hot pepper sauce
  1 17-ounce can cream-style corn
  1 16-ounce can whole white
     potatoes, drained and diced
  1 4½-ounce can shrimp, drained
  2 tablespoons snipped parsley
  1½ cups milk
  2 tablespoons all-purpose flour

Place bacon in a 2-quart casserole; cover with paper toweling. Micro-cook till crisp, about 3 minutes. Remove bacon; drain. Reserve 1 tablespoon drippings in casserole. Drain clams; reserve liquid. To reserved bacon drippings stir in reserved clam liquid, onion, hot pepper sauce, and ½ teaspoon salt. Cook, covered, till onion is tender, about 4 minutes. Stir in clams, corn, potatoes, shrimp, and parsley. Blend ¼ *cup* of the milk into flour; stir into soup with remaining milk. Cook, covered, till thickened and bubbly, about 10 minutes, stirring every 4 minutes. Before serving, sprinkle with bacon pieces. Makes 4 to 6 servings.

Lemony Ham and Rice Soup

In a 1½-quart casserole combine ¼ cup sliced green onion with tops and 1 tablespoon butter *or* margarine; micro-cook till tender, about 1½ minutes. Stir in 2 tablespoons all-purpose flour. Add one 10½-ounce can condensed chicken with rice soup, 1 soup can water, ½ cup finely chopped fully cooked ham, and 1 tablespoon lemon juice. Cook, covered, 8 minutes, stirring every 2 minutes. Sprinkle with freshly grated nutmeg. Makes 3 or 4 servings.

Tasty morsels of clam, shrimp, corn, potato, ▸ and bacon make *Seafood-Corn Chowder* a microwave hit for supper. Serve with crispy French bread slices toasted under the broiler.

Creamy Hamburger Chowder

    4 ounces ground beef
    ¼ cup finely chopped celery
    2 tablespoons finely chopped onion
    4 teaspoons all-purpose flour
    ¼ teaspoon salt
    ¼ teaspoon dried basil, crushed
    1½ cups milk
    ½ cup shredded sharp American
        cheese (2 ounces)
    1 tablespoon snipped parsley

In a 1½-quart casserole crumble ground beef. Add celery and onion. Micro-cook, covered, till meat is brown and vegetables are almost tender, about 4 minutes, stirring several times to break up meat. Drain off excess fat.

Blend flour, salt, and basil into meat. Stir in milk. Micro-cook, uncovered, till thickened and bubbly, about 5 minutes, stirring every 2 minutes. Stir in cheese till melted. Season to taste with additional salt and pepper. Sprinkle parsley over top. Makes 2 servings.

Cheesy Cauliflower Soup

    1 small head cauliflower, broken
        into flowerets and coarsely
        chopped (12 ounces)
    2 tablespoons sliced green
        onion with tops
    2 tablespoons water
    1½ cups chicken broth
    1 cup milk
    ½ teaspoon Worcestershire sauce
    2 tablespoons all-purpose flour
    ½ cup shredded sharp American
        cheese (2 ounces)
    Snipped chives

In a 1½-quart casserole combine cauliflower, green onion, and water. Micro-cook, covered, till tender, about 5 minutes, stirring once; do not drain. Stir in chicken broth, ¾ *cup* of the milk, and Worcestershire sauce.

Stir remaining ¼ cup milk into flour; stir into cauliflower mixture. Micro-cook, uncovered, till soup is slightly thickened and bubbly, 5 to 6 minutes, stirring after each minute. Stir in shredded cheese till melted. Before serving, sprinkle each serving with snipped chives. Makes 4 servings.

Vegetable-Cream Soup

    ½ cup chopped celery
    ¼ cup chopped onion
    2 tablespoons water
    1 10¾-ounce can condensed
        cream of mushroom soup
    1 10¾-ounce can condensed
        vegetable soup
    1 soup can milk (1¼ cups)
    ¼ teaspoon seasoned salt
    ½ cup dairy sour cream
    2 tablespoons snipped parsley

In a 1½-quart casserole combine celery, onion, and water. Micro-cook, covered, till vegetables are tender, about 5 minutes. Blend in soups, milk, and seasoned salt. Micro-cook, covered, just till boiling, 6½ to 7 minutes, stirring every 2 minutes. Blend in sour cream; micro-cook, covered, about 30 seconds.

To serve, sprinkle each serving with a little snipped parsley. Makes 4 servings.

From Leftovers to Croutons

Take your leftover bread, cut it into cubes, and turn the cubes into crispy soup or salad garnishes. Make them plain or add cheese for flavor.

Plain Croutons: Spread 4 cups ½-inch bread cubes (about 5 slices bread) in 12x7½-2-inch baking dish. Micro-cook, uncovered, till crisp and dry, about 6 to 7 minutes, stirring every 2 minutes. Store in tightly covered container. Makes 3 cups.

Cheese Croutons: Micro-melt 2 tablespoons butter in 12x7½x2-inch baking dish, 30 to 40 seconds. Add 4 cups ½-inch bread cubes, stirring to coat. Micro-cook, uncovered, till cubes begin to dry, about 2 minutes. Sprinkle with 2 tablespoons grated Parmesan cheese; mix well. Cook, uncovered, till croutons are crisp, about 6 minutes longer, stirring every 2 minutes. Store in tightly covered container. Makes 3 cups.

Medium White Sauce

   2 tablespoons butter *or* margarine
   2 tablespoons all-purpose flour
   ¼ teaspoon salt
      Dash pepper
   1 cup milk

In a 2-cup glass measure micro-melt the butter 30 to 40 seconds. With rubber scraper blend in flour, salt, and pepper; stir in milk till well blended. Micro-cook, uncovered, 1 minute; stir. Micro-cook till thickened and bubbly, 2 to 3 minutes; stir thoroughly every 30 seconds, scraping bottom and sides of cup to remove all lumps. Makes about 1 cup.

For Thick White Sauce: Prepare Medium White Sauce, *except* increase butter to 3 tablespoons and flour to ¼ cup. Makes 1 cup.

For Cheese Sauce: Prepare Medium White Sauce; stir in 1 cup shredded American cheese till melted. If necessary, micro-cook 30 seconds to melt cheese. Makes 1½ cups.

Cranberry-Orange Sauce

   1 pound fresh cranberries (4 cups)
   2 cups sugar
   ½ cup water
   1 teaspoon grated orange peel
   ½ cup orange juice
   ½ cup slivered almonds (optional)

In a 2-quart casserole combine all ingredients except nuts. Micro-cook, covered, till berries pop, about 12 minutes; stir after 6 minutes, then stir every 2 minutes. Stir in nuts. Chill in covered container. Makes 4 cups.

Easy Chasseur Sauce

In medium glass bowl micro-cook 2 tablespoons sliced green onion with tops in 2 tablespoons butter *or* margarine till tender, about 1½ minutes. Blend in 1 envelope brown gravy mix and 1 tablespoon tomato paste. Stir in ¾ cup water; ½ cup dry red wine; one 3-ounce can chopped mushrooms, drained; and ½ teaspoon dried fines herbes, crushed. Cook, uncovered, till thickened and bubbly, 3 minutes; stir every minute. Serve with beef. Makes 1¾ cups.

Mustard-Cream Sauce

   2 tablespoons butter *or* margarine
   3 tablespoons all-purpose flour
   1 teaspoon prepared mustard
   ¼ teaspoon salt
      Dash white pepper
   ¾ cup chicken broth
   ½ cup light cream *or* milk
      • • •
   2 teaspoons snipped chives
   1 teaspoon prepared horseradish
   1 teaspoon lemon juice

In a 1-quart casserole micro-melt the butter 30 to 40 seconds. Blend in flour, mustard, salt, and white pepper. Gradually stir in chicken broth and light cream or milk.

Micro-cook, uncovered, 1 minute; stir thoroughly. Micro-cook, uncovered, till sauce is thickened and bubbly, about 2 minutes longer, stirring every 30 seconds. Stir in snipped chives, horseradish, and lemon juice. Micro-cook, uncovered, 45 seconds more. Serve with baked fish, green vegetables, or hard-cooked eggs. Makes 1½ cups sauce.

French Onion Sauce

   2 large onions, thinly sliced and
      separated into rings (3 cups)
   2 tablespoons butter *or* margarine
      • • •
   2 tablespoons cold water
   2 tablespoons cornstarch
   1 10½-ounce can condensed
      beef broth
   ¼ teaspoon Worcestershire sauce
   2 tablespoons grated Parmesan
      cheese

In 1-quart casserole micro-cook onion in butter or margarine, covered, until onion is tender, about 5 minutes, stirring after 3 minutes. Stir the cold water into the cornstarch. Stir into cooked onion mixture. Blend in the beef broth and Worcestershire sauce. Micro-cook, uncovered, till mixture is thickened and bubbly, about 4½ to 5 minutes, stirring after each minute. Stir in the cheese. Micro-cook uncovered, 1 minute longer. Serve over meat loaf, ground beef patties, or on sliced roast beef atop French bread. Makes 2½ cups.

Hearty Sandwiches

*T*he Earl of Sandwich never dreamed that one day sandwiches would be prepared in a microwave oven. But you can pop all shapes, kinds, and sizes into your oven. In this section, look for variations of popular sandwiches plus some new ideas, too.

Spicy Meatball Sandwiches

      1 beaten egg
    ¼ cup milk
      1 cup soft bread crumbs
         (about 1½ slices)
    ¼ cup finely chopped onion
    ¾ teaspoon salt
      1 pound ground beef
         • • •
      1 clove garlic, crushed
      1 tablespoon butter *or* margarine
    ½ cup catsup
    ⅓ cup chili sauce
      2 tablespoons packed brown sugar
      1 tablespoon prepared mustard
      1 teaspoon Worcestershire sauce
      1 teaspoon celery seed
    ¼ teaspoon salt
         Few drops bottled hot
            pepper sauce
      6 hard rolls *or* frankfurter buns,
         split and toasted

In a mixing bowl combine egg, milk, bread crumbs, onion, and ¾ teaspoon salt. Add meat; mix well. Shape mixture into 18 meatballs; arrange in 10x6x2-inch baking dish. Micro-cook, covered, 9 minutes, turning and rearranging meatballs twice. Drain off fat.

In a 2-cup glass measure micro-cook garlic in butter 1 minute. Stir in catsup, chili sauce, brown sugar, mustard, Worcestershire sauce, celery seed, the remaining ¼ teaspoon salt, and hot pepper sauce. Micro-cook, uncovered, till mixture boils, about 2½ minutes, stirring twice. Pour sauce over meatballs. Micro-cook till sauce bubbles, about 2½ minutes, stirring twice. Serve meatballs with sauce in hard rolls. Makes 6 sandwiches.

Pizza Joes

If using Italian sausage for these sandwiches, shown on the cover, omit the salt and fennel—

      1 pound ground beef *or* bulk
         Italian sausage
    ¼ cup chopped onion
      1 8-ounce can pizza sauce
      2 tablespoons grated
         Parmesan cheese
    ½ teaspoon salt
    ¼ teaspoon fennel seed
    ¼ teaspoon garlic powder
      6 hard rolls *or* frankfurter buns
      6 slices mozzarella cheese (each
         about 3 inches square)

In glass bowl crumble meat; add onion. Micro-cook, covered, till meat is brown, 5 to 6 minutes; stir several times to break up meat. Drain. Stir in pizza sauce, Parmesan, salt, fennel, and garlic. Micro-cook, uncovered, till hot, about 3 minutes, stirring once.

Split rolls; divide and spoon hot filling atop bottom half of rolls. Top *each* with a cheese slice; cover with roll top. Place on a paper plate. Micro-cook, uncovered, till filling is hot and cheese starts to melt, 20 to 25 seconds for one roll, or 1 minute for six rolls, giving plate a half turn once. Makes 6.

Chicken Salad in a Roll

In a 4-cup glass measure combine 2 cups diced cooked chicken; ⅔ cup mayonnaise *or* salad dressing; one 3-ounce can chopped mushrooms, drained; ⅓ cup grated Parmesan cheese; ¼ cup finely chopped celery; 2 tablespoons snipped parsley; 1 tablespoon lemon juice; and ¼ teaspoon dried rosemary, crushed. Micro-cook chicken salad filling, uncovered, for 3 minutes, stirring mixture once.

Split 6 hard rolls. Divide and spoon hot filling atop bottom half of rolls; cover with tops. Wrap *each* roll in paper toweling. Cook till warm, about 30 seconds for one roll, or 1 minute for four to six rolls. Makes 6.

Egg Salad Sandwich Pizzas

RECIPE FOR **2**

2 hard-cooked eggs, chopped
¼ cup chopped pepperoni
2 tablespoons chili sauce
2 tablespoons mayonnaise *or*
   salad dressing
1 tablespoon finely chopped onion
⅛ teaspoon salt
⅛ teaspoon dried basil, crushed
   Dash garlic powder
   Dash pepper
2 English muffins, split
   and toasted
¼ cup shredded mozzarella
   cheese (1 ounce)

In a glass bowl combine chopped eggs, pepperoni, chili sauce, mayonnaise, onion, salt, basil, garlic powder, and pepper. Micro-cook, uncovered, till heated through, 1½ to 2 minutes, stirring once. Spread mixture on the four toasted muffin halves; sprinkle mozzarella cheese atop. Micro-cook, uncovered, till cheese melts, 30 to 60 seconds. Serves 2.

Ham and Pineapple Ring Sandwich

Shape ham patties to fit pineapple rings—

1 beaten egg
¾ cup soft bread crumbs (1 slice)
2 tablespoons finely chopped onion
½ pound ground fully cooked ham
1 8¼-ounce can sliced
   pineapple, drained
4 hamburger buns, split
   and toasted
   Butter *or* margarine
   Prepared mustard
4 lettuce leaves

Combine egg, soft bread crumbs, and onion. Add ham; mix well. Form into four patties slightly larger than pineapple rings. Make a hole in the center of *each* patty. In 12x7½x2-inch baking dish place ham patties atop pineapple rings. Micro-cook, covered, till meat is done, about 6 minutes, giving dish a half turn and turning patties over once.

Spread buns with butter and mustard. Place a ham patty and pineapple ring on bottom half of *each* bun; top with lettuce leaf, then bun top. Serve at once. Makes 4 sandwiches.

Yankee Codfish Rarebit

This main dish sandwich is shown on page 17—

8 ounces salted cod
¼ cup butter *or* margarine
3 tablespoons all-purpose flour
½ teaspoon dry mustard
   Dash cayenne
1¼ cups milk
½ teaspoon Worcestershire sauce
1 cup shredded sharp American
   cheese (4 ounces)
1 beaten egg
6 English muffins, split
3 tomatoes, sliced (12 slices)

Soak cod in water 12 hours, changing water once; drain. In a 1-quart casserole combine cod and enough water to cover (about 1 cup). Micro-cook, covered, till fish flakes easily, about 4½ minutes. Drain and dice cod.

In same casserole micro-melt the butter about 45 seconds. Blend in flour, mustard, and cayenne. Stir in milk and Worcestershire. Micro-cook, uncovered, 1 minute; stir. Cook till thickened and bubbly, about 2 minutes; stir every 30 seconds. Stir in cheese till melted. Gradually stir ½ *cup* of the hot mixture into egg; return to hot mixture. Cook, uncovered, 30 seconds; stir after 15 seconds. Stir in cod; cook, covered, till hot, about 2 minutes, stirring once. Toast muffins; top with tomatoes. Cover with sauce. Trim with parsley and paprika, if desired. Makes 6 servings.

Frank Reubens

8 slices pumpernickel *or*
   rye bread, toasted
½ cup Thousand Island
   salad dressing
6 frankfurters, split lengthwise
1 8-ounce can sauerkraut,
   well drained
4 slices Swiss cheese

Spread one side of toast with dressing. Top *each* of 4 toast slices with 3 frank halves, about *2 tablespoons* kraut, and *1* cheese slice. Top with remaining toast. Place on paper toweling. Micro-cook, uncovered, till cheese melts, about 1 minute for one sandwich, or 2½ minutes for four sandwiches. Makes 4.

Delectable Desserts

Now you can prepare quickly and effortlessly in your microwave oven some of those desserts that previously required spending much time in the kitchen. Look over this section for a selection of recipes—from crisps and cobblers to quick-to-make candies.

Apple-Cranberry Crisp

¼ cup granulated sugar
½ teaspoon cornstarch
⅓ cup fresh cranberries
2 tart apples, peeled, cored, and sliced
Several drops almond extract
2 tablespoons quick-cooking rolled oats
2 tablespoons packed brown sugar
1 tablespoon all-purpose flour
Dash ground cinnamon
1 tablespoon butter *or* margarine

RECIPE FOR 2

In a 1-quart casserole mix granulated sugar and cornstarch; gradually blend in 3 tablespoons cold water. Stir in berries. Micro-cook, covered, till berries pop, about 3 minutes, stirring once. Stir in apples and extract. Turn into two 1-cup glass baking dishes.

In mixing bowl combine oats, brown sugar, flour, and cinnamon. Cut in butter till crumbly. Sprinkle crumb mixture atop fruit in baking dishes. Micro-cook, uncovered, till apples are tender, about 3½ minutes, turning dishes twice. Serve warm. Makes 2 servings.

Granola Brown Betty

Peel, core, and slice 7 or 8 tart medium apples (6 cups). In large bowl combine apples, ⅓ cup apple juice, ¼ cup raisins, ¼ cup honey, 4 teaspoons all-purpose flour, and ½ teaspoon ground cinnamon. Turn into 10x6x2-inch baking dish. Micro-cook, covered, 12 minutes, turning dish every 2 minutes. Top with 1 cup granola cereal. Cook, uncovered, 1 minute. Serve with light cream. Serves 4 to 6.

Strawberry-Banana Cobbler

3 firm medium bananas
1 21-ounce can strawberry pie filling
1 tablespoon lemon juice
½ teaspoon vanilla
9 coconut bar cookies, crumbled (1 cup)
¼ cup chopped pecans
Vanilla ice cream *or* light cream

Peel and slice bananas; place in 10x6x2-inch baking dish. Mix pie filling, lemon juice, and vanilla; spoon over bananas. Micro-cook, uncovered, 6 minutes, turning dish every 2 minutes. Mix cookies and pecans; sprinkle over fruit. Cook, uncovered, 1 minute. Serve warm with ice cream or light cream. Serves 6.

Graham Cracker Bars

2 cups finely crushed graham crackers (29 square crackers)
⅔ cup sugar
3 tablespoons butter *or* margarine
½ cup semisweet chocolate pieces
¼ cup chopped nuts
1 5⅓-ounce can evaporated milk (⅔ cup)
1 teaspoon vanilla

In bowl mix crumbs and sugar; cut in butter till mixture resembles cornmeal. Stir in chocolate and nuts. Add milk and vanilla; mix well. Place a small juice glass in center of greased 8x8x2-inch baking dish; spread batter around glass. Micro-cook, uncovered, till top appears dry, about 7 minutes; give dish a quarter turn every 2 minutes. *Loosen edges; remove glass.* Cool. Cut into bars. Makes 24.

Be ready for requests for seconds when you ▸ offer *Strawberry-Banana Cobbler* topped with vanilla ice cream or light cream. Convenience ingredients plus microwave cooking make this dessert an excellent choice for those busy days.

Golden Fruit Compote

Drain one 13¼-ounce can pineapple tidbits, reserving ⅓ cup syrup. In 10x6x2-inch baking dish micro-melt 3 tablespoons butter *or* margarine 35 to 40 seconds; blend in reserved syrup, ¼ cup orange liqueur, 2 tablespoons packed brown sugar, and ⅛ teaspoon ground cinnamon. Drain one 11-ounce can mandarin orange sections and one 16-ounce can peach slices; stir fruits into butter mixture with pineapple. Micro-cook, uncovered, about 5 minutes; stir every 2 minutes. Stir in 1 medium banana, sliced; cook 1 minute. Serves 6.

Graham Cracker-Prune Pudding

Butterscotch Sauce
½ cup snipped pitted dried prunes
3 tablespoons sugar
2 tablespoons shortening
½ teaspoon vanilla
1 egg yolk
¼ cup chopped walnuts
1 cup finely crushed graham
    crackers (14 square crackers)
½ teaspoon baking powder
⅓ cup milk
1 stiffly beaten egg white

Butterscotch Sauce: In a 4-cup glass measure combine ½ cup packed brown sugar, 1 tablespoon cornstarch, and dash salt; mix well. Stir in ½ cup water and 2 tablespoons light corn syrup. Micro-cook, uncovered, till thickened and bubbly, 3 to 4 minutes; stir after each minute. Cook 1 minute more. Stir in 2 tablespoons butter *or* margarine. Cool 30 minutes *without stirring*. Makes about 1 cup.

Meanwhile, in 4-cup glass measure micro-cook 1 cup water till boiling, about 3½ minutes. Stir in prunes; let stand till cool. Drain.

In small mixing bowl cream sugar with shortening and vanilla. Add yolk; beat well. Stir in prunes and nuts. Mix crumbs with baking powder and ⅛ teaspoon salt. Add to creamed mixture alternately with milk. Fold in egg white. Divide among 4 greased 6-ounce custard cups. Arrange cups in oven, leaving space between cups. Micro-cook, uncovered, till done, about 4 minutes, rearranging twice. Serve warm with Butterscotch Sauce. Serves 4.

Apple Spice Cake

½ cup packed brown sugar
¼ cup butter *or* margarine,
    softened
1 egg
1 cup all-purpose flour
1 teaspoon baking powder
½ teaspoon ground cinnamon
¼ teaspoon ground ginger
¼ teaspoon ground cloves
½ cup milk
2 tart medium apples, peeled, cored,
    and thinly sliced (2 cups)
Crumb Topping
Whipped cream

Cream sugar and butter. Add egg; beat well. Stir flour with baking powder, spices, and ¼ teaspoon salt. Add to creamed mixture alternately with milk; beat after each addition. Spread in greased and floured 8x1½-inch round baking dish. Arrange apples over batter; sprinkle with Crumb Topping. Micro-cook, uncovered, about 7 minutes, giving dish a quarter turn every 2 minutes. Serve warm or cool. Cut in wedges; top with whipped cream.

Crumb Topping: Mix ¼ cup packed brown sugar, ¼ cup all-purpose flour, and ½ teaspoon ground cinnamon. Cut in 2 tablespoons butter till mixture resembles coarse crumbs.

Citrus Pudding Cake

In a 2-quart glass mixing bowl micro-melt 2 tablespoons butter 30 to 40 seconds. Blend in ¾ cup sugar; add 1 beaten egg. Mix well. Stir together 1 cup all-purpose flour, 1 teaspoon baking powder, and ½ teaspoon salt. Add to sugar mixture; stir till smooth. Stir in ⅔ cup water. Pour into ungreased 8x8x2-inch baking dish, spreading evenly; set aside.

In a 4-cup glass measure micro-cook 1 cup water and ½ cup orange juice till boiling, 4 to 4½ minutes. Add ¾ cup sugar and 3 tablespoons butter *or* margarine; stir till butter melts. Stir in 1 teaspoon grated lemon peel and 3 tablespoons lemon juice. Carefully pour over cake batter. Micro-cook, uncovered, till wooden pick inserted in center comes out clean, about 9 minutes; give dish a quarter turn every 3 minutes. Serve warm. Serves 6.

Cherry-Brownie Pudding Cake

    2 tablespoons butter
    1 21-ounce can cherry pie filling
    2 tablespoons lemon juice
    1 cup sugar
    ¼ cup butter, softened
    2 egg yolks
    ½ teaspoon vanilla
    2 1-ounce squares unsweetened
        chocolate, melted and cooled*
    ¼ cup milk
    1 cup all-purpose flour
    ½ teaspoon baking powder
    ½ teaspoon salt
    2 stiffly beaten egg whites
    ⅓ cup chopped walnuts

In a 4-cup glass measure micro-melt 2 table-spoons butter 30 to 40 seconds; stir in pie filling, lemon juice, and ⅓ cup water. Spread in 12x7½x2-inch baking dish; set aside.

Cream 1 cup sugar and ¼ cup butter together. Add yolks and vanilla; beat till fluffy. Stir in chocolate and milk. Mix flour, baking powder, and salt. Add to chocolate mixture; mix well. Fold in whites and nuts. Carefully spoon batter over cherry mixture. Micro-cook, uncovered, till wooden pick inserted in center comes out clean, about 13 minutes; give dish a half turn every 3 minutes. Serve warm with vanilla ice cream, if desired. Serves 8 to 10.

*See tip at right for melting chocolate.

Rice Pudding

    3 beaten eggs
    2 cups milk
    ⅓ cup sugar
    1 teaspoon vanilla
    ½ teaspoon salt
    2 cups cooked rice
    ⅓ cup raisins
      Ground cinnamon
      Light cream

In a 2-quart casserole combine eggs, milk, sugar, vanilla, and salt. Add rice and raisins; mix well. Micro-cook, uncovered, just till thickened, 8 to 10 minutes, stirring every 1½ to 2 minutes. Sprinkle with cinnamon. Let stand 30 minutes without stirring. Serve warm or chilled with light cream. Serves 6 to 8.

Melting Chocolate the Easy Way

Save messy cleanup by melting chocolate squares in their own paper wrappers. Place unwrapped squares, with folded side of wrapper up, in microwave oven. (Place in dish, if desired.) Micro-melt 2 minutes for 1 square, or 2½ to 3 minutes for 2 squares. Lift wrappers by folded ends.

Nesselrode Custard

    2 coconut macaroon cookies,
        crumbled (⅓ cup)
    2 tablespoons chopped mixed
        candied fruits and peels
    2 tablespoons chopped raisins
    1 beaten egg
    ⅔ cup milk
    2 tablespoons sugar
    ¼ teaspoon rum flavoring

Pour 2 cups water into an 8x8x2-inch baking dish. Micro-cook, uncovered, till hot, 4 to 4½ minutes. Meanwhile, mix first three ingredients; divide mixture and press lightly into two 6-ounce custard cups. Mix egg, milk, sugar, flavoring, and dash salt; pour into prepared cups. Set cups in hot water in baking dish. Micro-cook, uncovered, till almost set, about 7 minutes; give dish a quarter turn after each minute. Remove cups from water; let stand at least 15 minutes before serving. Serves 2.

Raisin-Filled Apples

    ⅓ cup raisins
    ¼ cup packed brown sugar
    2 tablespoons chopped walnuts
    ¼ teaspoon ground cinnamon
    4 large baking apples, cored

Mix the first four ingredients. Peel off a strip around top of apples. Place apples in 10x6x2-inch baking dish; fill centers with nut mixture. Micro-cook, covered, till tender, 5 to 6 minutes; give dish a half turn twice. Let stand 15 minutes before serving. Serves 4.

Cap your next company meal with a flaming dessert such as *Banana-Raspberry Flambé*. To reduce last-minute preparation, prepare sieved raspberry mixture earlier in the day. When dessert time arrives, slice bananas and micro-cook in sauce before adding the liqueur.

Banana-Raspberry Flambé

Do not overheat liqueur—heat just till warm enough to flame—

> **1 10-ounce package frozen red raspberries, thawed**
> **2 tablespoons granulated sugar**
> • • •
> **2 tablespoons butter *or* margarine**
> **1 tablespoon packed brown sugar**
> **4 medium bananas, sliced (1 to 1¼ pounds)**
> **3 tablespoons orange liqueur**
> **Vanilla ice cream**

In blender container place raspberries and granulated sugar; cover and blend till smooth. Sieve to remove seeds; set aside.

In 12x7½x2-inch baking dish micro-melt the butter 30 to 40 seconds. Stir in brown sugar till dissolved; stir in raspberry mixture and bananas, stirring to coat all slices. Cook, covered, till heated through and bananas are cooked, about 3½ minutes, stirring twice.

Add liqueur and cook 30 seconds more. *Or,* micro-heat liqueur in a 1-cup glass measure 30 seconds (*do not overheat*). Transfer liqueur to ladle. Carefully flame; pour over fruit. Serve over ice cream. Makes 2½ cups.

Jiffy Ice Cream Toppers

Do you avoid hot sundae toppings because of the extra heating step? Now, make hot fudge or butterscotch sundaes in a jiffy by simply placing the glass jar of topping, uncovered, in microwave oven till topping begins to heat. Serve at once over ice cream.

Scotch Crunchies

A quick sweet for a busy day (shown on cover)—

1 6-ounce package butterscotch
    pieces (1 cup)
1 6-ounce package semisweet
    chocolate pieces *or* imitation
    chocolate-flavored pieces
1 3-ounce can chow mein noodles
1 cup tiny marshmallows *or* raisins

In large glass bowl place butterscotch and chocolate pieces. Micro-cook, uncovered, till melted, about 2½ minutes; stir after each minute. Stir in noodles and marshmallows or raisins. Drop by teaspoon onto waxed paper. Chill, if desired. Makes about 3 dozen.

Chocolate-Nut Pillows

1 6-ounce package semisweet
    chocolate pieces (1 cup)
1 tablespoon shortening
½ cup peanut butter
2 tablespoons sifted powdered
    sugar
3 cups presweetened shredded
    wheat biscuits
1½ cups finely chopped peanuts
    or flaked coconut

In medium glass bowl place the chocolate and shortening. Micro-cook, uncovered, till melted, about 2½ minutes; stir after each minute. Stir in peanut butter and sugar till smooth. Halve wheat biscuits crosswise. Using fork, dip biscuits in chocolate mixture; lift and draw off excess against rim of bowl. Roll in nuts or coconut. Dry on waxed paper. Makes 40 to 42.

Easy Opera Fudge

This simple fudge is shown on the cover—

½ cup butter *or* margarine
2 3- or 3¼-ounce packages *regular*
    vanilla pudding mix
½ cup milk
½ teaspoon vanilla
1 16-ounce package sifted powdered
    sugar (about 4¾ cups)
⅓ cup nuts *or* candied cherries,
    chopped

In 2-quart glass bowl micro-melt the butter about 1 minute. Stir in dry mix and milk. Micro-cook, uncovered, till boiling, about 3 minutes; stir occasionally. Cook 1 minute more, stirring every 15 seconds. Add vanilla. Beat in sugar; stir in nuts or cherries. Pour into buttered 10x6x2-inch baking dish. Top with nut halves, if desired. Chill; cut in 1-inch squares. Store in refrigerator. Makes 2 pounds.

Smoothie Chocolate Fudge

1 6-ounce package semisweet
    chocolate pieces (1 cup)
½ cup *sweetened condensed* milk
1 cup sifted powdered sugar
½ teaspoon vanilla
    Dash salt
⅓ cup chopped walnuts

In 1-quart glass bowl combine chocolate and milk. Micro-cook, covered, until chocolate melts, about 1 minute, stirring once. Stir in sugar, vanilla, and salt. Fold in the nuts. Turn into waxed paper-lined 8½x4½x2½-inch loaf pan. Let stand till set. Turn out; cut in pieces. Makes about 1 pound fudge.

Peanut Butter S'Mores

For *each* s'more spread 1 graham cracker square with about 2 teaspoons peanut butter. Top with about 9 semisweet chocolate pieces and about 6 tiny or 1 large marshmallow. Cover with another graham cracker square; wrap loosely in paper toweling. Micro-cook till chocolate and marshmallows melt, about 1 minute for one s'more, or 1 to 1½ minutes for four s'mores.

Meals Prepared by Microwave

Everyone welcomes more spare time, whether it's time to read the evening paper before starting dinner or time for a favorite hobby. Your microwave oven will give you that extra time by cutting minutes off mealtime preparations. Learn how to dovetail the micro-cooking sequence of food. Remember that you can interrupt the preparation of one dish to prepare another or use the range top simultaneously. With each of the menus on the next few pages you'll find a suggested cooking sequence to help you prepare the meals.

Use cooking times as guidelines since countertop microwave ovens vary by manufacturer. See tip box on page 6 for information regarding recipe timings.

Surprise your family with a Creole dinner. Cook the *Bread and Butter Pudding*, *Spicy Sauce*, and the *Creole-Style Chicken* in the microwave oven. (See Index for page numbers.) Meanwhile, prepare the rice and okra on top of the range.

Brunches and Breakfasts

WEEKEND BRUNCH

Spicy Fruit Trio
Eggs Buckingham
Buttered Asparagus Spears
Beverage

Preparation Sequence: Prepare fruit compote first and let stand at room temperature or chill. Micro-cook beef sauce for egg entrée. Meanwhile, cook asparagus spears according to package directions on top of the range. Micro-cook eggs, then assemble main dish and place in the microwave oven till heated through. Drain and butter asparagus spears.

Spicy Fruit Trio

Serve this colorful fruit compote either warm or chilled in your prettiest sherbet dishes—

  1 8¾-ounce can unpeeled
       apricot halves
  ¼ cup water
  4 whole cloves
  4 inches stick cinnamon
  2 oranges, peeled and sectioned
  1 cup sliced fresh strawberries
     Fresh mint sprigs

Drain apricot halves, reserving syrup; cut up apricots. In a 1-quart casserole combine reserved apricot syrup, water, whole cloves, and stick cinnamon. Micro-cook, covered, for 3 minutes; mixture will boil. Stir in apricots; micro-cook, covered, 2 minutes more. Let stand, covered, at room temperature 20 to 30 minutes; or, chill, if desired.

Remove cloves and stick cinnamon and discard. Stir in orange sections and strawberries. Spoon fruit mixture into sherbets; garnish with mint sprigs and a whole sliced strawberry, if desired. Makes 4 servings.

Eggs Buckingham

  3 tablespoons butter *or* margarine
  2 tablespoons all-purpose flour
     Dash pepper
  1¼ cups milk
  1 3-ounce package sliced smoked
       beef, snipped (1 cup)
       • • •
  1 tablespoon butter *or* margarine
  4 eggs
  1 tablespoon milk
     Dash salt
     Dash pepper
       • • •
  4 large rusks, buttered (each
       about 4 inches in diameter)

In a 2-cup glass measure micro-melt the 3 tablespoons butter or margarine 35 to 40 seconds. Blend in all-purpose flour and dash pepper. Thoroughly stir in the 1¼ cups milk. Micro-cook, uncovered, 1 minute; stir. Cook till thickened and bubbly, 2 to 3 minutes more, stirring sauce every 30 seconds to remove all lumps. Stir in snipped smoked beef; cover surface of sauce and set aside.

In a 9-inch glass pie plate micro-melt the 1 tablespoon butter or margarine 30 to 40 seconds. In a small bowl beat eggs with the 1 tablespoon milk, dash salt, and dash pepper. Pour beaten egg mixture into pie plate with the melted butter. Micro-cook, covered, till eggs are slightly softer than desired for scrambled eggs, 2½ to 3 minutes, stirring through entire mixture every 30 seconds.

Arrange buttered rusks on serving plate. Divide and spoon egg mixture over rusks; cover with beef sauce. Micro-cook, covered, till heated through, 1 to 1¼ minutes for four servings. Serve immediately. Makes 4 servings.

Extend a cheery hello to late-morning guests ▶ with this tasty brunch featuring *Spicy Fruit Trio*, *Eggs Buckingham*, asparagus spears, and plenty of hot coffee. Microwave cooking speeds the preparation of the compote and the entrée.

Menu

SPECIAL-DAY BRUNCH

Fresh Raspberries or Blueberries
Eggs à la Benedict
Coffee Cake
Beverage

Preparation Sequence: Rinse and lightly sugar the berries; chill till serving time. Begin preparation of scrambled eggs. Heat Canadian bacon in microwave oven and complete making sauce in blender. As egg entrée is assembled, micro-heat a purchased coffee cake.

Menu

BRUNCH ON THE PATIO

Grapefruit Halves
Sausage Patties   Fried Eggs
Graham Cracker Upside-Down Cake
Beverage

Preparation Sequence: Prepare upside-down cake and place in microwave oven. Begin pan frying sausage patties on range top. Meanwhile, halve and section grapefruit. When sausage is done, fry eggs in same skillet. Remove cake from oven; let cool slightly.

Eggs à la Benedict

1 tablespoon butter *or* margarine
4 eggs
2 tablespoons milk
4 slices Canadian-style bacon,
     cut ¼ inch thick (6 ounces)
½ cup butter *or* margarine
3 egg yolks
2 tablespoons lemon juice
     Dash cayenne
4 rusks, buttered

In a 1-quart casserole micro-melt 1 tablespoon butter 30 to 40 seconds. Beat whole eggs with milk, dash salt, and dash pepper; pour into casserole with melted butter. Micro-cook, covered, till of desired doneness, about 2 minutes; stir through entire mixture every 30 seconds. Cover and set aside.

Wrap Canadian bacon in waxed paper; place ½ cup butter in a 2-cup glass measure. Micro-cook bacon and butter till butter is bubbly and bacon is hot, about 1 minute. Remove from oven; do not unwrap bacon. In blender container combine yolks, lemon juice, and cayenne. Cover; quickly turn blender on and off. Then blend at high speed for about 30 seconds while slowly adding hot butter till fluffy.

To assemble, place a rusk on each plate; top each with a Canadian bacon slice. Spoon eggs over; spoon some of the sauce over eggs. Garnish with parsley, if desired. Serves 4.

Graham Cracker Upside-Down Cake

1 cup granulated sugar
½ cup butter *or* margarine
3 eggs
2 cups finely crushed graham
     crackers (28 square crackers)
1 teaspoon baking powder
¾ cup milk
½ cup packed brown sugar
2 tablespoons all-purpose flour
½ teaspoon ground cinnamon
2 tablespoons butter *or* margarine
½ cup chopped walnuts
     Vanilla ice cream

In large mixing bowl cream granulated sugar with ½ cup butter. Add eggs, one at a time; mix well after each, beating a total of about 5 minutes. Mix crumbs, baking powder, and ¼ teaspoon salt. Add to creamed mixture alternately with milk; set aside.

Combine brown sugar, flour, and cinnamon; cut in 2 tablespoons butter till crumbly. Stir in nuts. Spread *half* of the batter in greased 8x1½-inch round baking dish. Sprinkle evenly with *half* of the sugar mixture. Repeat with remaining batter and sugar mixture.

Micro-cook, uncovered, 10 minutes; give dish a quarter turn every 2 minutes. Surface will appear moist. Cool in dish. To serve, invert on serving plate; cut into wedges. Top with vanilla ice cream. Makes 6 to 8 servings.

Menu

SCHOOL-DAY BREAKFAST

Tomato Juice
Oatmeal with Peach-Orange Sauce
Crisp Bacon
Beverage

Preparation Sequence: Micro-cook oatmeal; cover and keep warm till serving time. Assemble sauce ingredients and place in microwave oven. As sauce cooks, layer bacon with paper toweling in baking dish; micro-cook till crisp. Pour juice; serve oatmeal in bowls.

Menu

BREAKFAST FOR SIX

Orange Juice
Double Corn and Ham Bake
Applesauce or Maple-Flavored Syrup
Beverage

Preparation Sequence: Combine applesauce ingredients in casserole; place in microwave oven. As sauce cooks, prepare corn bread batter and spread in baking dish. Set applesauce aside and micro-cook the corn bread; remove from oven. Meanwhile, pour juice.

Oatmeal with Peach-Orange Sauce

Served over hot cereal, this delicately flavored fruit sauce takes the place of sugar and cream—

>   3 cups water
> 1½ cups quick-cooking rolled oats
>   ½ teaspoon salt
> • • •
>   1 8¾-ounce can peach slices
>   2 tablespoons packed brown sugar
>   2 teaspoons cornstarch
>   ⅛ teaspoon ground cinnamon
>   Dash salt
>   ½ cup orange juice

In a 2-quart casserole stir together the water, quick-cooking rolled oats, and ½ teaspoon salt. Micro-cook, uncovered, till cereal mixture boils, about 5 minutes, stirring twice. Remove cereal from oven and cover to keep hot while preparing the fruit sauce.

To prepare fruit sauce, drain peach slices, reserving syrup. Chop sliced peaches; set aside. In a 4-cup glass measure combine the packed brown sugar, cornstarch, ground cinnamon, and dash salt. Stir in orange juice and reserved peach syrup. Micro-cook, uncovered, till mixture is heated through, about 2 minutes. Micro-cook 3 minutes longer, stirring sauce after each minute. Stir in chopped peaches. To serve, spoon hot oatmeal into cereal bowls; pass warm sauce for spooning over cereal. Makes 4 or 5 servings.

Double Corn and Ham Bake

Top this quick bread with micro-baked applesauce or warmed maple-flavored syrup—

>   3 medium apples, peeled, cored,
>   and chopped (3 cups)
>   ¼ cup water
>   3 tablespoons packed brown sugar
>   1 tablespoon lemon juice
>   ¼ teaspoon ground cinnamon
> • • •
> 1½ cups finely chopped
>   fully cooked ham
>   1 8¾-ounce can cream-style corn
>   1 8-ounce package corn muffin mix
>   1 beaten egg

In a 1½-quart casserole combine apples, water, brown sugar, lemon juice, and cinnamon; micro-cook, covered, till apples are very soft, 6 to 7 minutes, stirring once or twice. Mash apples slightly, if desired. Cover; set aside.

Combine ham, corn, dry muffin mix, and egg; mix well. Place a small juice glass upright in center of greased 8x1½-inch round baking dish; spread corn batter around glass. Micro-cook, uncovered, till wooden pick inserted halfway between center and edge comes out almost clean, about 9 minutes, giving dish a quarter turn every 3 minutes. Let stand a few minutes; remove juice glass. Cut into wedges; serve topped with applesauce or warmed maple-flavored syrup, if desired. Serves 6

Lunch-Time Menus

BUSY-DAY LUNCH

Ham and Applewiches
or
Tuna Open-Facers
Potato Chips
Sweet Pickles   Celery Sticks
Chocolate-Swirled Pudding
Beverage

Preparation Sequence: Make pudding and chill. Clean celery and set out pickles and potato chips. Prepare either sandwich. Toast bread as the sandwich filling heats.

Chocolate-Swirled Pudding

¾ **cup sugar**
2 **tablespoons cornstarch**
¼ **teaspoon salt**
2 **cups milk**
1 **beaten egg**
2 **tablespoons butter** *or* **margarine**
1 **teaspoon vanilla**
4 **teaspoons fudge topping**
4 **teaspoons peanut butter**
   (optional)
2 **tablespoons chopped peanuts**

In a 4-cup glass measure mix sugar, cornstarch, and ¼ teaspoon salt; slowly stir in milk. Micro-cook, uncovered, 3 minutes; stir. Cook for 2 to 2½ minutes until thickened and bubbly, stirring after each minute. Stir a moderate amount of hot mixture into egg; return to hot mixture. Cook, uncovered, till bubbly, about 1 minute. Stir in butter and vanilla. Spoon into individual dessert dishes. Top *each* with *1 teaspoon* of the fudge topping and *1 tea-spoon* of the peanut butter, if desired; swirl with knife. Top with nuts. Chill. Serves 4.

Ham and Applewiches

4 **slices boiled ham**
4 **spiced apple rings, drained**
4 **slices American cheese, halved**
   diagonally (4 ounces)
¼ **cup mayonnaise** *or* **salad dressing**
1 **teaspoon prepared mustard**
4 **slices white** *or* **rye bread,**
   toasted

Place ham on waxed paper in microwave oven; top with apple rings. Micro-cook, covered, till hot, 1 to 1½ minutes for four ham slices, or 30 to 45 seconds for one. Uncover; top *each* with *2* half slices cheese. Cook till cheese melts, about 1 minute for four sandwiches, or 20 to 30 seconds for one. Mix mayonnaise and mustard; spread over one side of toast. Place ham atop toast. Makes 4 sandwiches.

Tuna Open-Facers

1 **6½- or 7-ounce can tuna,**
   drained and flaked
¼ **cup mayonnaise** *or* **salad dressing**
¼ **cup chopped green pepper**
2 **tablespoons sweet pickle relish**
2 **tablespoons chopped onion**
4 **slices white bread, toasted**
4 **slices American cheese**

In a 1-quart glass bowl mix first 5 ingredients. Micro-cook, uncovered, 3 minutes; stir after each minute. (For one sandwich, cook ⅓ cup filling 30 seconds; stir. Cook 15 seconds.) Spread hot filling on toast. Top *each* sandwich with cheese slice. Place sandwiches on waxed paper in microwave oven. Cook four sandwiches, uncovered, 1 minute. Rearrange; cook till cheese melts, 30 seconds. (For one sandwich, melt cheese 20 to 30 seconds.) Makes 4.

Lunch-in-a-hurry is a frequent challenge for ▶ many families. Next time you hear such a request, serve this colorful lunch of hot *Ham and Applewiches* and *Chocolate-Swirled Pudding*.

SUMMER LUNCH

Bacon-Cheese Rarebit
Pickle Slices   Carrot Curls
Nut Bars or Taffy Baked Apples
Beverage

Preparation Sequence: Bake the dessert first; cool while preparing the remainder of the lunch. Prepare carrot curls and chill in ice water. Set out pickles. Combine ingredients for cheese sauce as bacon cooks in microwave oven. While cheese sauce cooks, toast and butter the English muffins. Heat tomatoes; assemble sandwiches.

Bacon-Cheese Rarebit

Sharp American cheese makes this open-face sandwich a favorite of cheese fans—

> 4 slices bacon, halved
> 1 beaten egg
> 2 cups shredded sharp American
>   cheese (8 ounces)
> ¾ cup milk
> 1 teaspoon dry mustard
> 1 teaspoon Worcestershire sauce
>   Dash cayenne
>   • • •
> 4 tomato slices
> 2 English muffins, split,
>   toasted, and buttered

In shallow baking dish or on paper plate place bacon between layers of paper toweling. Micro-cook till crisp, 3½ to 4 minutes. Set aside. In a 1-quart casserole combine egg, cheese, milk, dry mustard, Worcestershire sauce, and cayenne. Micro-cook, uncovered, till cheese melts and sauce thickens, 4 to 5 minutes, stirring after each minute.

In shallow baking dish or paper plate micro-heat tomato slices, uncovered, 30 seconds. To assemble, place *1* tomato slice and *2* bacon pieces atop *each* toasted and buttered muffin half; pour cheese sauce over all. Serve immediately. Makes 4 sandwiches.

Taffy Baked Apples

Spicy molasses sauce coats these apples—

> ⅓ cup sugar
> ⅓ cup water
> ¼ cup molasses
> 2 tablespoons lemon juice
> ½ teaspoon ground cinnamon
> ½ teaspoon ground nutmeg
>   Dash ground cloves
>   Dash ground ginger
> 4 medium cooking apples

In small bowl combine sugar, water, molasses, lemon juice, ground cinnamon, ground nutmeg, ground cloves, and ground ginger. Remove cores from apples; peel strip from top of each apple. In an 8-inch glass pie plate place apples, top-side down. Pour molasses mixture over apples. Micro-cook, uncovered, for 4 minutes. Turn apples, top-side up, and rearrange. Cook till apples are tender, about 4 minutes more. Cool slightly before serving. Makes 4 servings.

Nut Bars

A chewy sweet for dessert or snacks—

> 2 tablespoons butter *or* margarine
> 1 cup packed brown sugar
> 1 cup chopped nuts
> ⅓ cup all-purpose flour
> ⅛ teaspoon baking soda
> ⅛ teaspoon salt
> 2 beaten eggs
> 1 teaspoon vanilla
>   Powdered sugar

In 8x8x2-inch baking dish micro-melt the butter or margarine 30 to 40 seconds. In mixing bowl thoroughly stir together the brown sugar, chopped nuts, all-purpose flour, baking soda, and salt; stir in beaten eggs and vanilla. Carefully pour nut mixture over melted butter in baking dish; do not stir.

Micro-cook, uncovered, till done, 6 to 6½ minutes, giving dish a quarter turn after each minute. Cookies will appear moist in the center. Remove from oven; let stand 2 minutes.

Sift powdered sugar over top of cookies. Place waxed paper under wire rack; invert cookies onto rack. Cool. Dust again with powdered sugar. Cut into bars. Makes 24.

Menu

SOUPER LUNCH

Hearty Hodgepodge
or
Cheesy Chicken Soup
Assorted Crackers
Rhubarb Crisp   Vanilla Ice Cream
Beverage

Preparation Sequence: Assemble ingredients for dessert and bake in the microwave oven. As the dessert cools, prepare either of the soups. During the final cooking of the soup, place the crackers in a basket.

Rhubarb Crisp

A springtime favorite topped with ice cream—

> 3 cups rhubarb cut in ½-inch
>   pieces (1 pound)
> ¼ to ⅓ cup packed brown sugar
> 1 tablespoon cornstarch
> ⅔ cup water
> 1 teaspoon vanilla
> ½ teaspoon grated lemon peel
> • • •
> ⅓ cup all-purpose flour
> ¼ cup packed brown sugar
> ½ teaspoon ground cinnamon
> 2 tablespoons butter *or* margarine
>   Vanilla ice cream

Place rhubarb in 8x1½-inch round baking dish; set aside. In a 2-cup glass measure combine ¼ to ⅓ cup packed brown sugar and cornstarch; stir in water till blended. Micro-cook, uncovered, till mixture thickens and bubbles, 2 to 3 minutes, stirring after each minute. Stir in vanilla and lemon peel. Pour sauce over rhubarb in baking dish; stir lightly.

In small bowl combine all-purpose flour, ¼ cup packed brown sugar, and ground cinnamon. Cut in butter or margarine till crumbly; sprinkle over rhubarb mixture. Micro-cook, uncovered, till rhubarb is tender, about 10 minutes, turning dish once. Serve warm with vanilla ice cream. Makes 4 servings.

Hearty Hodgepodge

> ¼ cup finely chopped celery
> ¼ cup finely chopped onion
> ½ pound ground beef
> ⅛ teaspoon garlic powder
> 1 10¾-ounce can condensed
>   minestrone soup
> 1 soup can water (1¼ cups)
> 1 8-ounce can pork and beans
>   in tomato sauce
> 1 teaspoon Worcestershire sauce
> 1 teaspoon beef-flavored
>   gravy base
> ¼ teaspoon dried oregano, crushed

In small glass bowl combine celery and onion; micro-cook, covered, till vegetables are tender, about 4 minutes. Set aside.

In 1½-quart casserole crumble ground beef; add garlic powder. Micro-cook, covered, till meat is brown, about 3 minutes, stirring several times to break up meat. Drain off excess fat. Stir in celery-onion mixture, condensed minestrone soup, water, pork and beans in tomato sauce, Worcestershire sauce, beef-flavored gravy base, and oregano. Micro-cook, covered, till mixture bubbles, about 5 minutes, stirring twice. Makes 4 servings.

Cheesy Chicken Soup

> 1 whole small chicken breast,
>   halved lengthwise (8 ounces)
> ½ cup water
> ¼ cup chopped onion
> ¼ cup chopped carrot
> ¼ cup chopped celery
> 1 10½-ounce can condensed
>   cream of chicken soup
> ¾ cup milk
> ½ cup shredded sharp American
>   cheese (2 ounces)

In 1½-quart casserole combine chicken, water, onion, carrot, and celery. Micro-cook, covered, till chicken and vegetables are tender, about 7 minutes. Remove chicken; cool slightly. Discard skin and bones; cut up meat. Return chicken to casserole. Stir in condensed soup; blend in milk. Micro-cook, uncovered, till hot, 4 to 5 minutes, stirring once. Stir in cheese till melted. Makes 4 servings.

Dinners for the Family

Menu

MEAT LOAF SPECIAL

Beef and Mushroom Loaf
Bean Pot Peppers
or
Peas and Celery Especiale
Cottage Cheese-Tomato Salad
Hard Rolls   Butter
Chocolate Cakelettes
or
Apple-Rice Pudding
Beverage

Preparation Sequence: Mix ingredients for either of the desserts. As the dessert cooks, prepare the salad and begin preparation of either of the vegetable dishes. Make meat loaf mixture; shape and micro-cook. Complete cooking vegetable while meat loaf rests.

Beef and Mushroom Loaf

> 1 beaten egg
> 3 tablespoons milk
> 1 3-ounce can chopped
>   mushrooms, drained
> ¼ cup quick-cooking rolled oats
> 2 tablespoons snipped parsley
> 1 teaspoon onion salt
>   • • •
> 1 pound ground beef
> ½ cup shredded sharp American
>   cheese (2 ounces)

In bowl combine first 6 ingredients. Add beef; mix well. In a 9-inch glass pie plate shape mixture into a 7x1-inch round loaf. Micro-cook, covered, 5 minutes; drain off fat. Micro-cook, uncovered, till done, about 2 minutes more. Sprinkle with cheese. Micro-cook till cheese melts, 45 to 60 seconds. Let stand 5 minutes; transfer to serving platter. Makes 4 servings.

Bean Pot Peppers

> 2 large green peppers
>   Salt
> 1 14-ounce can pork and beans in
>   molasses sauce
> ⅓ cup finely crushed gingersnaps
>   (5 cookies)
> 1 tablespoon instant minced onion
> 1 tablespoon packed brown sugar
> 2 teaspoons Worcestershire sauce
> 1 teaspoon prepared mustard

Halve peppers lengthwise; remove seeds and membranes. Place peppers in a 10x6x2-inch baking dish. Micro-cook, covered, for 2 minutes. Sprinkle insides of peppers with salt.

In mixing bowl combine beans in molasses sauce, gingersnap crumbs, instant minced onion, brown sugar, Worcestershire sauce, and prepared mustard; mix well. Spoon bean mixture into the four pepper halves. Micro-cook, uncovered, till beans are heated through, about 4 minutes. Garnish with quartered gingersnaps, if desired. Makes 4 servings.

Peas and Celery Especiale

> 1 cup bias-sliced celery
> 1 8-ounce can tomato sauce
> 2 tablespoons chopped onion
> ½ teaspoon salt
> ⅛ teaspoon dried oregano, crushed
>   Dash pepper
> 1 10-ounce package frozen peas
> 1 tablespoon cold water
> 1 teaspoon cornstarch

In 1½-quart casserole combine celery, tomato sauce, onion, salt, oregano, and pepper. Micro-cook, covered, 7 minutes, stirring once. Stir in peas. Micro-cook, covered, till peas are done, about 5 minutes, stirring twice.

Stir cold water into cornstarch; blend into vegetable mixture. Micro-cook, uncovered, till mixture is thickened and bubbly, about 1½ minutes, stirring twice. Serve vegetables in sauce dishes. Makes 4 servings.

Oven meals are quick and easy to prepare when you use a microwave oven. By dovetailing mixing and cooking steps, the oven meal shown above including cheesy *Beef and Mushroom Loaf, Bean Pot Peppers*, and *Chocolate Cakelettes*, is ready to serve on short order.

Chocolate Cakelettes

⅔ cup all-purpose flour
½ cup sugar
3 tablespoons unsweetened
   cocoa powder
1 teaspoon baking powder
⅛ teaspoon salt
⅓ cup water
1 beaten egg
¼ cup cooking oil
½ teaspoon vanilla
¼ cup semisweet chocolate pieces
  Whipped cream *or* whipped topping

In a mixing bowl stir together flour, sugar, cocoa powder, baking powder, and salt. Stir in water, egg, oil, and vanilla; mix thoroughly. Stir in chocolate pieces. Spoon batter into six greased 6-ounce custard cups. Micro-cook three cakes at a time, uncovered, till wooden pick comes out clean, about 2 minutes. Loosen edges of cakes; remove from dishes. If desired, serve warm. Top with whipped cream or whipped topping. Makes 6 cupcakes.

Apple-Rice Pudding

1 cup apple cider *or* apple juice
¾ cup chopped apple
   (peeled, if desired)
1 tablespoon butter *or* margarine
1 tablespoon sugar
¼ teaspoon salt
  Dash ground cinnamon
⅔ cup Minute Rice
    ● ● ●
1 cup frozen whipped dessert
   topping, thawed
  Ground nutmeg

In 1½-quart casserole combine apple cider or apple juice, chopped apple, butter, sugar, salt, and ground cinnamon. Micro-cook, covered, till mixture bubbles, about 3½ minutes. Stir in rice. Cover and let stand for 5 minutes to absorb liquid; fluff mixture with a fork. Place in the refrigerator to chill.

Just before serving, fold in whipped dessert topping. Spoon into dessert dishes. Sprinkle with ground nutmeg. Makes 4 servings.

Menu

WEEKDAY DINNER

Vegetable-Burger Cups
Sliced Tomatoes
Tossed Salad   Italian Dressing
or
Crisp Relishes
Bread Sticks   Butter
Red Berry Sundaes
Beverage

Preparation Sequence: Prepare dessert sauce for sundaes; place in the refrigerator to chill till dessert time. Slice tomatoes, prepare salad or relishes, and set out bread sticks. Combine ingredients for meat mixture and shape over cups. Prepare vegetable sauce. When sauce is cooked, place meat cups in microwave oven to cook. Then, reheat the vegetable sauce in the meat cups.

Menu

SATURDAY SUPPER

Pork Chow Mein
Chow Mein Noodles
Buttered Peas
Cabbage Salad
or
Waldorf Salad
Fruity Tapioca
Beverage

Preparation Sequence: Earlier in the day, prepare pudding; cool before folding in fruits and marshmallows. Chill. Begin meal preparation by making one of the salads; cover and refrigerate. Assemble main dish ingredients. As pork chow mein cooks in the microwave oven, cook peas on range top. During final cooking of main dish, butter cooked peas.

Vegetable-Burger Cups

To mold meat, shape over inverted custard cups—

> 1 beaten egg
> ¼ cup milk
> ⅓ cup coarsely crushed saltine crackers (9 crackers)
> ½ envelope sloppy joe seasoning mix (2 tablespoons)
> 1 pound ground beef
> 2 medium carrots, peeled and thinly sliced (1 cup)
> 1 cup fresh or frozen peas
> ¼ cup chopped onion
> ½ teaspoon instant beef bouillon granules
> 1 tablespoon all-purpose flour
> ½ cup shredded American cheese

Mix first 4 ingredients. Add beef; mix well. On 4 squares waxed paper pat meat into four 5-inch rounds. Shape each over an inverted 6-ounce custard cup; discard paper. Place inverted cups in 12x7½x2-inch baking dish. Cover; set aside. In 1-quart casserole combine carrots, peas, onion, bouillon granules, ¾ cup water, and dash pepper. Micro-cook, covered, till vegetables are tender, about 10 minutes, stirring once. Stir ¼ cup cold water into flour; blend into vegetables. Cook, uncovered, till thickened and bubbly, about 1 minute. Stir in cheese till melted. Cover; set aside.

Micro-cook meat cups, covered, 3 minutes; give dish a half turn. Cook, covered, till almost done, about 2 minutes more. Lift meat cups from custard cups; place on serving platter. Fill with vegetable sauce. Cook, uncovered, till sauce is hot, 1 to 2 minutes. If desired, garnish with raw onion rings and parsley sprigs. Makes 4 servings.

Red Berry Sundaes

In 1-quart glass bowl micro-defrost one 10-ounce package frozen red raspberries, uncovered, 2 minutes. Add ½ cup orange juice. Mix ¼ cup sugar and 1 tablespoon cornstarch; stir into berries. Micro-cook, uncovered, till thickened and bubbly, about 4½ minutes, stirring after each minute. Cook 1 minute more. Stir in 1 cup halved fresh strawberries. Chill. Serve over vanilla ice cream. Makes 2½ cups.

A delicate cheese sauce dresses fresh-from-the-garden vegetables in hearty *Vegetable-Burger Cups*. Shaped over inverted custard cups, the meat loaf mixture is baked in the microwave oven, then filled with a vegetable sauce. A final heating makes them piping hot.

Pork Chow Mein

   2 tablespoons butter *or* margarine
   1 pound boneless pork,
       cut in small cubes
1½ cups sliced celery
   1 cup chopped onion
   1 cup chicken broth
   1 tablespoon molasses
¼ cup soy sauce
   2 tablespoons cornstarch
   1 16-ounce can bean
       sprouts, drained
   Chow mein noodles

In 2-quart casserole micro-melt the butter 30 to 40 seconds; add pork, celery, and onion. Micro-cook, uncovered, till meat is cooked and vegetables are tender, about 12 minutes, stirring every 2 minutes. Stir in broth and molasses. Stir soy into cornstarch; blend into pork mixture. Cook, uncovered, till thickened and bubbly, about 2½ to 3 minutes, stirring after each minute. Stir in sprouts. Cook, uncovered, till hot, about 1½ minutes, stirring twice. Serve over noodles. Serves 4.

Fruity Tapioca

This colorful pudding is pictured on the cover—

   1 8¾-ounce can peach slices
       Milk
   1 3¼-ounce package *regular* orange
       tapioca pudding mix
   1 tablespoon lemon juice
½ cup tiny marshmallows
   2 tablespoons sliced
       maraschino cherries

Drain peaches, reserving syrup; set 4 slices aside for garnish. Dice remaining peaches. Add milk to reserved peach syrup to equal 2 cups liquid. In a 4-cup glass measure combine the dry pudding mix with the milk-syrup mixture. Stir till pudding mix is dissolved. Micro-cook, uncovered, 3 minutes; stir. Micro-cook, uncovered, till thickened and bubbly, 3 to 4 minutes more, stirring every 30 seconds. Stir in lemon juice; cool 45 minutes.

Fold diced peaches, marshmallows, and maraschino cherries into pudding; chill. Spoon pudding into sherbet dishes; garnish with reserved peach slices. Makes 4 servings.

FAMILY DINNER

Ham Medley
Parsleyed Carrots
Lettuce Wedge   Vinegar-Oil Dressing
Apple-Gingerbread Cobbler
Beverage

Preparation Sequence: Start by cooking noodles for the casserole on range top. Bake cobbler and cupcakes. While the dessert cools, cut lettuce wedges for the salad and micro-cook carrots till tender; set aside. Prepare the ham casserole; micro-cook casserole and let stand while preparing sauce for carrots. Reheat carrots with sauce. If necessary, micro-heat the cobbler just before serving.

Ham Medley

        2 cups medium noodles (3 ounces)
    ¾ cup chopped celery
    ½ cup chopped onion
    ¼ cup chopped green pepper
        3 tablespoons butter *or* margarine
        3 tablespoons all-purpose flour
    ½ teaspoon dried dillweed
        1 cup milk
        1 cup cream-style cottage cheese
        2 cups cubed fully cooked ham
        2 tablespoons butter *or* margarine
    ⅓ cup fine dry bread crumbs

On Range Top: Cook noodles in boiling salted water following package directions; drain.

In 2-quart casserole combine celery and next 3 ingredients. Micro-cook, covered, till tender, 3 minutes. Blend in flour, dill, ¼ teaspoon salt, and ⅛ teaspoon pepper. Stir in milk and cheese. Micro-cook, uncovered, till thickened and bubbly, 4 to 4½ minutes, stirring after each minute. Stir in noodles and ham. Micro-cook, uncovered, till hot, about 6 minutes, stirring twice. Let stand 5 minutes.

In a 1-cup glass measure micro-melt 2 tablespoons butter 30 to 40 seconds; stir in crumbs. Sprinkle atop casserole. Serves 6.

Parsleyed Carrots

        6 to 9 carrots, sliced ⅛ inch
            thick (3 cups)
    ⅓ cup water
        1 tablespoon butter *or* margarine
    ½ teaspoon lemon juice
    ¼ teaspoon salt
    ⅛ teaspoon paprika
        2 tablespoons snipped parsley

In a 1-quart casserole combine carrots and ⅓ cup water. Micro-cook, covered, till carrots are tender, about 9 minutes; drain. Stir butter or margarine, lemon juice, salt, and paprika into carrots. Micro-cook, covered, till heated through, about 1 to 2 minutes. Stir in snipped parsley. Makes 6 servings.

Apple-Gingerbread Cobbler

        4 medium apples, peeled, cored,
            and sliced (4 cups)
        1 cup water
    ¼ cup packed brown sugar
        1 tablespoon lemon juice
    ¼ teaspoon ground cinnamon
                ● ● ●
        1 tablespoon cold water
        2 teaspoons cornstarch
        1 14-ounce package gingerbread mix
            Whipped cream

In 1½-quart casserole combine apples, 1 cup water, brown sugar, lemon juice, and cinnamon. Micro-cook, covered, till apples are tender, about 6½ to 7 minutes, stirring once.

Blend 1 tablespoon cold water into cornstarch; stir into apple mixture. Micro-cook, uncovered, till thickened and bubbly, 1½ minutes, stirring twice. Turn into 12x7½x2-inch baking dish. Prepare gingerbread mix following package directions. Pour *1 cup** of the batter evenly over apple mixture. Micro-cook, uncovered, till wooden pick comes out clean, about 5 minutes, giving dish a half turn after 2½ minutes. Serve warm with whipped cream. Makes 8 servings.

*Note: To bake remaining batter, fill paper bake cup-lined 6-ounce custard cups half full (about 3 tablespoons). Micro-cook four at a time, uncovered, till done, 1½ to 2 minutes, rearranging cups once. Makes 8 cupcakes.

CREOLE DINNER

Creole-Style Chicken
Fluffy Rice   Buttered Okra
Frozen Fruit Salad
Bread and Butter Pudding
Bourbon Sauce or *Spicy Sauce*
Beverage

Preparation Sequence: Micro-cook the dessert and one of the sauces; set aside. Prepare the chicken in the microwave oven. Meanwhile, cook the rice and okra on range top. Arrange the salad on serving plates; stir butter into okra.

Creole-Style Chicken

This peppery dish is pictured on page 52—

> **2 slices bacon**
> **¼ cup chopped onion**
> **1 small clove garlic, crushed**
> **1 16-ounce can tomatoes, cut up**
> **2 cups cubed cooked chicken**
> **¼ cup coarsely chopped**
>   **green pepper**
> **1 teaspoon instant beef**
>   **bouillon granules**
> **Few dashes bottled**
>   **hot pepper sauce**
> **1 tablespoon cornstarch**
> **Hot cooked rice**

In 1½-quart casserole place bacon; cover with paper toweling. Micro-cook till crisp, 2 to 2½ minutes. Drain bacon, leaving drippings in casserole. Crumble bacon; set aside.

In reserved drippings micro-cook onion and garlic, uncovered, till tender, about 2 minutes. Stir in undrained tomatoes, next 4 ingredients, and ¼ teaspoon salt. Micro-cook, covered, till bubbly, about 5 to 6 minutes, stirring twice. Stir 1 tablespoon cold water into cornstarch; stir into hot mixture. Micro-cook, covered, till bubbly, 3 to 4 minutes, stirring after each minute. Cook 1 minute more. Sprinkle with bacon. Serve over rice. Serves 4.

Bread and Butter Pudding

This homespun dessert is shown on page 52—

> **2 tablespoons butter *or* margarine**
> **2 eggs**
> **1 cup milk**
> **⅓ cup sugar**
> **¼ cup raisins**
> **1 teaspoon vanilla**
> **1½ cups day-old French bread**
>   **cut in 1-inch cubes**
> **Bourbon Sauce *or* Spicy Sauce**
>   **(see recipes below)**

In a 1-quart casserole micro-melt the butter 30 to 40 seconds. Add eggs; beat well. Blend in milk, sugar, raisins, vanilla, and ⅛ teaspoon salt. Stir in bread cubes. Let stand 5 minutes; stir gently. Micro-cook, uncovered, till set, about 5½ to 6 minutes, stirring after 3 minutes. Serve warm with Bourbon Sauce or Spicy Sauce. Makes 4 servings.

Bourbon Sauce

> **½ cup sugar**
> **1 tablespoon cornstarch**
> **¾ cup water**
> **2 tablespoons butter *or* margarine**
> **2 tablespoons bourbon**

In a 4-cup glass measure stir together sugar and cornstarch; stir in water. Micro-cook, uncovered, till thickened and bubbly, about 3 minutes, stirring after each minute. Cook 1 minute more. Stir in butter and bourbon. Serve warm. Makes about 1¼ cups sauce.

Spicy Sauce

> **½ cup sugar**
> **1 tablespoon cornstarch**
> **½ teaspoon ground cinnamon**
> **½ teaspoon ground nutmeg**
> **2 tablespoons butter *or* margarine**
> **½ teaspoon vanilla**

In a 4-cup glass measure mix sugar, cornstarch, and spices; stir in ¾ cup water. Micro-cook, uncovered, till thickened and bubbly, about 3 minutes, stirring after each minute. Cook 1 minute more. Stir in butter and vanilla. Serve warm. Makes about 1 cup sauce.

Special Company Meals

Menu

DINNER FOR SIX

Ham Veronique
Stuffed Sweet Potatoes
Buttered Peas
Bibb Lettuce and Tomato Salad
Cloverleaf Rolls   Butter
Hot Fudge-Rum-Pecan Sundaes
Wine   Coffee

Preparation Sequence: Assemble ingredients for sundae sauce and toast pecans; set aside till dessert time. Micro-bake sweet potatoes. Meanwhile, prepare the salad; chill. Mash sweet potatoes while the ham heats in the microwave oven and peas cook on the range top. Make sauce for ham. Finish micro-cooking potatoes. Micro-heat the rolls.

Ham Veronique

> 1 1½- to 2-pound fully cooked ham slice, cut 1 inch thick
> 2 tablespoons sugar
> 2 teaspoons cornstarch
> ¾ cup rosé wine
> 1 tablespoon sliced green onion
> • • •
> ¾ cup seedless green grapes, halved (4 ounces)

Place ham in a 12x7½x2-inch baking dish. Micro-cook, covered, till heated through, about 8 minutes, giving dish a half turn after 4 minutes. Drain; cover and set aside.

In a 2-cup glass measure combine sugar and cornstarch; stir in wine and onion. Micro-cook, uncovered, till thickened and bubbly, about 2 to 2½ minutes, stirring after each minute. Stir in grapes; spoon over ham. Micro-cook, uncovered, 1 minute. Transfer ham to serving platter, topping with sauce. Serves 6.

Stuffed Sweet Potatoes

Select 6 medium sweet potatoes of approximately the same size and shape (7 to 8 ounces each). Scrub; prick well with fork. In microwave oven arrange potatoes on paper toweling, allowing at least 1 inch between potatoes. Micro-cook, uncovered, till potatoes are done, about 17 to 19 minutes; halfway through cooking time, rearrange potatoes.

Cut slice from top of each potato; carefully scoop out inside. Reserve shells. In mixing bowl combine potatoes, 3 tablespoons butter *or* margarine, 1 tablespoon packed brown sugar, ½ teaspoon salt, ⅛ teaspoon ground nutmeg, and dash pepper. Beat with electric mixer or rotary beater till fluffy, adding enough milk to moisten. Pile into shells; top with ¼ cup chopped pecans, if desired. Place on serving plate. Micro-cook, uncovered, till hot, about 3 to 4 minutes. If desired, brush shells with melted butter. Makes 6 servings.

Hot Fudge-Rum-Pecan Sundaes

> ½ cup semisweet chocolate pieces
> 2 tablespoons milk
> ½ cup tiny marshmallows
> 2 tablespoons light rum
> • • •
> Vanilla ice cream
> Pecan halves, toasted

In a 2-cup glass measure combine chocolate pieces and milk. Micro-cook, uncovered, till chocolate is melted, about 2 minutes, stirring once. Stir in marshmallows and rum.

To serve, scoop vanilla ice cream into sherbets. Top with some hot fudge sauce, then sprinkle with a few toasted pecan halves (see tip, page 36). Makes ¾ cup sauce.

Seedless green grapes glisten in wine-sauced ▶ *Ham Veronique.* Appealing to the eye as well as the palate, this micro-cooked entrée adds a distinctive note to any dinner party.

Menu

Parsley Loaf

> **1 loaf frozen white bread dough**
> **2 tablespoons butter *or* margarine**
> **2 tablespoons snipped parsley**
> **Butter *or* margarine, melted**

In a 4-cup glass measure micro-cook 3 cups water till boiling, about 7 to 8 minutes. Place frozen loaf in greased 9x5x3-inch loaf dish. Place dish plus the cup of boiling water in microwave oven. Micro-cook, uncovered, 30 seconds. Let bread and water stand in oven 20 minutes with power off. Repeat cooking and standing step two times or till bread is thawed.

On lightly floured surface roll dough to 12x8½-inch rectangle. In a small glass bowl micro-melt the 2 tablespoons butter 30 to 40 seconds. Spread over dough; sprinkle with parsley. Roll up jelly-roll fashion, starting from narrow side; seal edges. Place, seam side down, in same greased loaf dish. Brush with a little water. Place, uncovered, in microwave oven with same measuring cup of hot water. Micro-cook 30 seconds. Let stand in oven 20 minutes. Repeat cooking and standing steps once more till bread is almost double.

Make shallow slashes atop loaf. In *conventional oven:* Bake at 375° till done, about 35 minutes. Brush top with melted butter. Remove from loaf dish; cool. Makes 1 loaf.

Party Chicken

Sprinkle one side of 4 whole small chicken breasts, skinned and boned (2½ pounds), with ½ teaspoon salt, ½ teaspoon paprika, and ⅛ teaspoon pepper. In 1-quart glass bowl micro-cook 2 tablespoons chopped onion in 2 tablespoons butter till tender, about 1½ minutes. Stir in 1½ cups dry bread cubes, ½ teaspoon salt, ¼ teaspoon poultry seasoning, and dash pepper. Add ¼ cup water; toss to moisten. Place about ⅓ *cup* stuffing on unseasoned side of each breast; fold breast over stuffing. Skewer with wooden picks.

In 10x6x2-inch baking dish micro-melt 1 tablespoon butter 30 to 40 seconds. Arrange chicken in dish; turn to coat with butter. Micro-cook, covered, till done, about 15 minutes; after 8 minutes, turn chicken and rearrange. Remove from oven; keep covered. Prepare Mushroom Sauce; spoon over chicken. Top with snipped parsley. Makes 4 servings.

Mushroom Sauce: In a 4-cup glass measure micro-cook ¼ cup chopped onion in 1 tablespoon butter *or* margarine till tender, about 1½ minutes. Stir in 1 tablespoon all-purpose flour, ½ teaspoon salt, and dash pepper; blend in ⅔ cup milk. Micro-cook, uncovered, 1 minute; stir. Micro-cook till thickened and bubbly, about 30 seconds, stirring once. Stir sauce into ½ cup dairy sour cream; return all to glass measure. Stir in two 3-ounce cans sliced mushrooms, drained. Micro-cook, uncovered, till hot, about 1 to 1½ minutes, stirring every 30 seconds. Makes 2 cups.

Cinnamon-Baked Pears

> **¼ cup red cinnamon candies**
> **1 cup apple cider *or* apple juice**
> **2 ripe large pears**
> **Whipped cream cheese**
> **1 tablespoon chopped walnuts**

In 8-inch glass pie plate micro-melt candies in cider, about 5 minutes. Peel, halve, and core pears; place, cut side down, in syrup. Micro-cook, covered, till tender, about 6 minutes; give dish a quarter turn every 2 minutes. Chill. To serve, spoon pears, cut side up, with syrup into dishes. Top each with a dollop of cheese and sprinkle with nuts. Serves 4.

Mℯⁿʋ

CONTINENTAL SUPPER

Meatball Carbonade
Hot Cooked Noodles
French-Style Green Beans
Fresh Spinach Salad
Assorted Relishes
Dinner Rolls   Butter
Raspberry-Topped Cheese Cups
Beverage

Preparation Sequence: Make dessert ahead; chill. Prepare meatballs and micro-cook. Cook noodles and beans on range top. Micro-cook sauce for meat and finish cooking meatballs. Prepare salad. Set out relishes and rolls.

Raspberry-Topped Cheese Cups

    2 3-ounce packages cream cheese
    ⅓ cup sugar
    1 envelope unflavored gelatin
    1 cup dairy sour cream
    ¼ teaspoon finely shredded lemon
        peel
    1 tablespoon lemon juice
    ¼ teaspoon almond extract
    ½ cup frozen whipped dessert
        topping, thawed
    Raspberry Sauce

Place cheese on paper plate; cut into pieces. Soften in microwave oven about 30 seconds. In 4-cup glass measure mix sugar, gelatin, and ¼ teaspoon salt. Stir in 1 cup water. Micro-cook, uncovered, till gelatin dissolves, about 1½ minutes; stir once. Stir in cheese, sour cream, lemon peel and juice, and extract; beat smooth. Fold in topping. Pour into six 6-ounce custard cups. Chill till firm, 3 to 4 hours. Unmold; spoon Raspberry Sauce over. Serves 6.

Raspberry Sauce: Thaw and sieve one 10-ounce package frozen red raspberries. In 2-cup glass measure mix ¼ cup sugar and 2 teaspoons cornstarch. Blend in fruit. Micro-cook, uncovered, 2 minutes; stir. Cook till bubbly, 1½ to 2 minutes more; stir every 30 seconds. Chill.

Meatball Carbonade

    2 slices bacon
    1 beaten egg
    1 cup beef broth
    ⅓ cup fine dry bread crumbs
    ¾ teaspoon salt
    ½ teaspoon Worcestershire sauce
        Dash pepper
    1 pound ground beef
            • • •
    2 medium onions, thinly sliced
        (1 cup)
    2 tablespoons butter *or* margarine
    2 tablespoons all-purpose flour
    ½ cup beer
    1 teaspoon packed brown sugar
    1 teaspoon vinegar
    1 teaspoon beef-flavored
        gravy base
    ½ teaspoon dried thyme, crushed
    ¼ teaspoon salt
        Dash pepper
    2 tablespoons snipped parsley
        Hot cooked noodles

Place bacon between layers of paper toweling in 12x7½x2-inch glass baking dish. Micro-cook till crisp, 1½ to 1¾ minutes; crumble and set aside. Remove paper toweling. Drain any excess fat from dish; set dish aside. Combine egg, *3 tablespoons* of the beef broth, bread crumbs, ¾ teaspoon salt, Worcestershire sauce, and dash pepper. Add ground beef; mix thoroughly. Shape meat mixture into 34 small meatballs, about ¾ inch in diameter. Place in the 12x7½x2-inch baking dish. Micro-cook, covered, till brown, about 5 minutes, rearranging meatballs twice. Discard fat; set meat aside.

In 1½-quart casserole combine onion and butter or margarine. Micro-cook, covered, till onion is tender, about 6 minutes, stirring every 2 minutes. Blend in flour. Add remaining beef broth, beer, brown sugar, vinegar, beef-flavored gravy base, thyme, ¼ teaspoon salt, and dash pepper. Micro-cook, uncovered, till mixture thickens and bubbles, 5 minutes, stirring three times. Stir in meatballs. Micro-cook covered, till meatballs are done, 5 to 6 minutes, stirring once. Before serving, top with crumbled bacon and snipped parsley. Let mixture stand several minutes before serving. Serve with hot cooked noodles. Makes 4 to 6 servings.

Menu

SEAFOOD SUPPER

Tomato Juice Cocktail
Seafood Thermidor
Asparagus Elegante
Lemon Gelatin Salad
Hard Rolls   Butter
Jiffy Pots de Creme
or
Plum-Orange Compote
White Wine
Cardamom Coffee Demitasse

Preparation Sequence: Prepare salad ahead; chill. Prepare dessert; chill. if desired. Micro-thaw fish; cook in seasoned broth. Complete the thermidor except for the final cooking. Meanwhile, cook asparagus in microwave oven. During final cooking of thermidor, add mushroom sauce ingredients to asparagus. While asparagus reheats, pour juice and unmold salad. Prepare demitasse after dinner.

Asparagus Elegante

Toasted sesame seed adds crunch—

>   2 8-ounce packages frozen
>   cut asparagus
>   Salt
>   Pepper
>   1 3-ounce can sliced
>   mushrooms, drained
>   2 tablespoons butter *or* margarine
>   1 teaspoon lemon juice
>   ½ teaspoon sesame seed, toasted

In a 1½-quart casserole place frozen cut asparagus. Micro-cook, covered, till asparagus is tender, about 10 minutes, stirring twice. Drain thoroughly. Season asparagus to taste with a little salt and pepper. Gently stir drained sliced mushrooms, butter or margarine, and lemon juice into asparagus. Micro-cook, covered, just till vegetables are heated through, about 2 minutes longer, stirring once. Turn asparagus into serving bowl; sprinkle with toasted sesame seed. Makes 4 to 6 servings.

Seafood Thermidor

>   1 pound fresh *or* frozen
>   cod fillets
>   1 small onion, quartered
>   1 lemon slice
>   1 10½-ounce can condensed
>   cream of shrimp soup
>   3 tablespoons all-purpose flour
>   ½ cup milk
>   ¼ cup shredded process Monterey Jack
>   cheese (1 ounce)
>   2 tablespoons snipped parsley
>   1 tablespoon butter *or* margarine
>   ½ cup soft bread crumbs
>   2 tablespoons grated
>   Parmesan cheese
>   ½ teaspoon paprika

Partially thaw fish, if frozen. (Micro-cook 2 minutes; let rest 2 minutes. Cook 1 minute. Turn fish over once.) Discard skin and bones, if present; cut fish into ½-inch cubes.

In a 1-quart casserole micro-cook onion and lemon in 1 cup water, covered, till boiling, about 2½ minutes; add fish. Micro-cook, covered, till fish flakes easily with a fork, about 3 minutes. Remove fish with slotted spoon; set aside. Discard cooking liquid.

In same casserole combine soup and flour; gradually stir in milk. Micro-cook, uncovered, till thickened and bubbly, about 4 minutes, stirring after each minute. Stir in shredded cheese and parsley; micro-cook, uncovered, till cheese melts, about 30 seconds. Fold in fish. If desired, transfer to 4 baking shells.

In a 1-cup measure micro-melt the butter 30 to 40 seconds; toss with crumbs, Parmesan, and paprika. Sprinkle atop casserole or shells. Micro-cook, uncovered, till edges are bubbly, about 2 to 3 minutes, turning dish once. Trim with parsley, if desired. Makes 4 servings.

Cardamom Coffee Demitasse

In a 4-cup glass measure mix 5 teaspoons instant coffee crystals and ⅛ teaspoon ground cardamom; stir in 2 cups water. Micro-cook, uncovered, just till bubbly, about 4 minutes; stir. Pour into demitasse cups. Top each with a dollop of frozen whipped dessert topping, thawed. Makes 4 (4-ounce) servings.

Parmesan-buttered bread crumbs dot *Seafood Thermidor* in individual baking shells. Cooked in the microwave oven, this delicate cod and shrimp bake is equally appropriate served in a single casserole dish. Offer a white wine with this elegant entrée for a very special dinner.

Jiffy Pots de Crème

A good make-ahead dessert for company meals—

 1 3¾- *or* 4-ounce package *regular*
    chocolate-fudge pudding mix
 2¼ cups milk
 ½ cup semisweet chocolate pieces
 1 teaspoon vanilla
    Sliced almonds, toasted

In a 4-cup glass measure combine the dry chocolate-fudge pudding mix and milk. Micro-cook, uncovered, for 3 minutes; stir. Micro-cook till bubbly, about 3 minutes longer, stirring every 30 seconds. Immediately add semisweet chocolate and vanilla to pudding; stir till chocolate pieces are melted. Cover surface of pudding with waxed paper; cool.

   Spoon cooled pudding into pots de crème cups; cover and chill. Before serving, garnish each dessert with a few toasted almonds (see tip, page 36). Makes 4 to 6 servings.

Plum-Orange Compote

 12 to 14 fresh Italian purple
    plums (1 pound)
 1 11-ounce can mandarin orange
    sections
 ½ cup sugar
 1 tablespoon lemon juice
 ¼ teaspoon ground cinnamon
 ⅛ teaspoon ground mace
    Dairy sour cream

Quarter or halve plums; discard pits. Drain oranges, reserving ¼ cup syrup. Set fruits aside. In 2-quart casserole mix sugar, lemon juice, spices, reserved syrup, and ¼ cup water. Micro-cook, covered, till boiling, about 2½ to 3 minutes; stir once. Stir in plums. Micro-cook, covered, just till tender, about 4 minutes; stir once. Fold in oranges. Cook 1 minute. Serve warm or chilled with sour cream. Sprinkle with ground mace, if desired. Serves 4 to 6.

Microwave Plus

Microwave plus what? you ask. Recipes using the microwave oven along with another appliance or piece of equipment, is an easy answer. In this section look for ideas using the microwave oven in combination with your regular range. Learn to use the microwave appliance with the freezer for make-ahead dishes. Discover the combination of micro-cooking and barbecuing over charcoal. Also check this section for recipes that use special features found on some microwave models, such as the defrost setting or browning unit.

Use cooking times as guidelines since countertop microwave ovens vary by manufacturer. See tip box on page 6 for information regarding recipe timings.

Use the freezer as the "plus" appliance for making *Date-Rice Dessert,* the conventional range for preparing *Cinnamon-Nut Ring* and *Spanish Chicken and Rice,* and a special browning dish for *Veal Parmesan.* (See Index for page numbers.)

Microwave Plus the Range

Team the microwave oven with the range—the oven, surface units, or broiler—for a winning cooking combination. Prepare part of the recipe by microwave and use conventional heat for tasks such as baking breads, cooking pasta, frying in fat, preparing crepes, and browning.

Cinnamon-Nut Ring

A yeast coffee cake shown on page 74—

> 1 loaf frozen white bread
>   dough (1 pound)
> 2 tablespoons butter, melted
> ⅓ cup packed brown sugar
> ¼ cup chopped walnuts
> 1 teaspoon ground cinnamon
>   Confectioners' Icing
>   Walnut halves

In a 4-cup glass measure micro-cook 3 cups water till boiling, about 7 to 8 minutes. Place loaf of frozen bread dough in greased 9-inch glass pie plate. Place pie plate in oven along with the measuring cup of water. Micro-cook, uncovered, 30 seconds. Let bread and water stand in oven 20 minutes with power off. Repeat cooking and standing step two times or until bread is thawed.

Roll thawed dough out on lightly floured surface to 13x9-inch rectangle; spread with melted butter. Combine brown sugar, chopped walnuts, and cinnamon; sprinkle over dough. Roll up jelly-roll fashion starting at long side; seal seam. Form into ring with seam side down in the greased 9-inch pie plate; seal ends together. Place in microwave oven with measuring cup of hot water. Cook 30 seconds. Let stand in oven 20 minutes with power off. Repeat once more till ring is almost double.

In Conventional Oven: Bake at 375° till done, about 20 minutes. Remove from pie plate. Cool. Drizzle Confectioners' Icing over top. Trim with walnut halves. Makes 1 coffee cake.

Confectioners' Icing: Combine ½ cup sifted powdered sugar, 1 teaspoon light corn syrup, ¼ teaspoon vanilla, and enough milk to make of drizzling consistency (about 1 tablespoon).

Beefy Spaghetti

> 12 ounces spaghetti
> 1 pound ground beef
> ½ cup finely chopped onion
> 1 clove garlic, minced
> 1 16-ounce can tomatoes, cut up
> 1 6-ounce can tomato paste
> 1 6-ounce can chopped mushrooms
> ¼ cup snipped parsley
> 1 tablespoon packed brown sugar
> 1 teaspoon dried oregano,
>   crushed
> ¾ teaspoon salt
>   Few dashes bottled hot pepper
>   sauce
>   Grated Parmesan cheese

On Range Top: In large saucepan cook spaghetti in large amount of boiling salted water till tender. Drain and keep hot.

Meanwhile, in 2-quart casserole crumble ground beef; add onion and garlic. Micro-cook, covered, till onion is tender and meat is brown, about 5 minutes, stirring several times to break up meat. Drain off excess fat. Stir in tomatoes, tomato paste, mushrooms with liquid, parsley, brown sugar, and seasonings.

Micro-cook, uncovered, till sauce is of desired consistency, about 10 minutes. Serve over hot spaghetti. Pass cheese. Serves 6.

Warm Breads in a Jiffy

It takes less than a minute to warm dinner rolls. Place rolls in a paper napkin-lined basket or plate. (The napkin absorbs excess moisture.) For one or two rolls, test after 15 seconds of micro-cooking. Do *not* overcook, since breads become tough when micro-cooked too long. Increase time slightly for additional rolls. Serve the heated rolls at once.

This family-pleasing *Enchilada Casserole* gets its peppy flavor from the canned enchilada sauce and jalapeño bean dip. For those who prefer their Mexican-style foods highly seasoned, use the "hot" enchilada sauce or add several dashes of hot pepper sauce to the cheese sauce.

Enchilada Casserole

- 12 corn tortillas
  Cooking oil
- 3 tablespoons all-purpose flour
- ½ teaspoon salt
- ¼ teaspoon paprika
- 1½ cups milk
- 1 10-ounce can mild enchilada sauce
- 1 cup shredded Cheddar cheese
- ½ cup sliced pitted ripe olives
- ¾ pound ground beef
- ½ cup chopped onion
- 1 10½-ounce can jalapeño bean dip
- 1 large tomato, chopped (¾ cup)

On Range Top: In medium skillet dip tortillas, one at a time, in small amount of hot cooking oil just till limp, but not crisp, about 5 to 10 seconds for each. Drain tortillas well on paper toweling; set aside.

In 4-cup glass measure combine flour, salt, and paprika. Stir in milk and enchilada sauce till blended. Micro-cook, uncovered, 2 minutes; stir. Cook till bubbly, about 4 to 5 minutes, stirring after each minute. Stir in cheese and olives till cheese melts; set sauce aside.

In glass bowl crumble beef; add onion. Micro-cook, covered, till meat is brown, about 5 minutes, stirring several times to break up meat. Drain off fat. Stir in bean dip, ½ teaspoon salt, and ⅛ teaspoon pepper; mix well. On *each* tortilla place about ⅓ cup meat mixture and *1 tablespoon* tomato; roll up tightly. Place seam side down in 12x7½x2-inch baking dish. Pour cheese sauce over; micro-cook, uncovered, till hot, 10 minutes. Give dish half turns every 4 minutes. Makes 4 servings.

Chinese Beef

 1 pound beef round steak
 2 tablespoons cooking oil
 2 teaspoons instant beef
   bouillon granules
 1 small head cauliflower, broken
   into flowerets (3 cups)
 ¼ cup chopped onion
 3 tablespoons soy sauce
 1 clove garlic, minced
 3 tablespoons cornstarch
 1 6-ounce package frozen pea pods
   Chow mein noodles

Cut meat across grain into thin slices 2 inches long. *On Range Top:* In skillet quickly brown *half* of meat at a time in hot oil; set aside.

In 2-quart casserole dissolve bouillon granules in 1½ cups hot water. Stir in cauliflower, onion, soy sauce, garlic, and browned beef. Micro-cook, covered, 5 minutes, stirring once. Blend ¼ cup cold water into cornstarch; stir into casserole. Micro-cook, covered, 3 minutes, stirring after each minute. Meanwhile, pour hot tap water over pea pods to thaw; drain. Stir pea pods into casserole. Micro-cook, covered, 2½ minutes, stirring once. Serve over chow mein noodles. Serves 6.

Crepes

 1½ cups milk
 1 cup all-purpose flour
 2 eggs
 1 tablespoon sugar
 ⅛ teaspoon salt

Beat all ingredients together till smooth. Lightly grease a 6-inch skillet or crepe pan.
On Range Top: Heat pan; remove from heat. Spoon in about *2 tablespoons* batter. Rotate pan so batter spreads evenly. Return to heat. Brown on one side only. To remove crepe, invert pan over paper toweling. Repeat to make 16 crepes, lightly greasing pan occasionally.

◀ **Utilize your kitchen appliances** to good advantage. Use the range top to prepare the *Crepes.* Then, stir together the yogurt filling and microcook the sauce. Put all the parts together and you have a special dessert—*Cherry Crepes.*

Cherry Crepes

   Crepes
 1 cup yogurt
 ¾ cup sugar
 ½ teaspoon ground cinnamon
 2 tablespoons cornstarch
 2 cups cranberry juice cocktail
 1 16-ounce can pitted tart red
   cherries, drained
 ½ teaspoon grated lemon peel
 ¼ teaspoon vanilla
   Few drops red food coloring

On Range Top: Prepare and bake Crepes.
Combine yogurt, ½ *cup* of the sugar, and cinnamon; spread on unbrowned sides of crepes. Roll up jelly-roll fashion. Place in 12x7½x2-inch baking dish. (Form two layers to prevent crowding.) In a 4-cup glass measure combine remaining sugar and cornstarch. Stir in cranberry juice, cherries, and remaining ingredients. Micro-cook, uncovered, till thickened and bubbly, about 5 to 7 minutes, stirring after each minute. Spoon over crepes in dish. Micro-cook, covered, till crepes are hot, about 4 minutes, turning dish once. Serves 6 to 8.

Chicken and Broccoli Crepes

On Range Top: Prepare and bake Crepes.
Place one 10-ounce package frozen chopped broccoli and 2 tablespoons water in 12x7½x2-inch baking dish. Micro-cook, covered, till done, 7 to 8 minutes, stirring once. Drain.

In bowl combine cooked broccoli, 2 cups finely chopped cooked chicken, ¼ cup shredded sharp American cheese, and 2 tablespoons chopped canned pimiento. Using two 10¾-ounce cans condensed cream of mushroom soup, spoon ¾ *cup* into the broccoli mixture; mix well. Spoon ¼ *cup* filling down the center of unbrowned side of each crepe. Roll up jelly-roll fashion. Place, seam side down, in 12x7½x2-inch baking dish. (Form two layers to prevent crowding.) Micro-cook, covered, till hot, about 12 minutes; turn dish twice.

In 4-cup glass measure mix remaining soup, ½ cup shredded sharp American cheese, and ¼ cup milk. Micro-cook, uncovered, till bubbly, 5 minutes; stir four times. Pour 1½ cups sauce over crepes. Pass remaining. Serves 8.

Spanish Chicken and Rice

A colorful and hearty main dish shown on page 75 —

> 6 chicken thighs (1½ pounds)
> 2 tablespoons cooking oil
>   Paprika
> ¾ pound ground beef
> ½ teaspoon salt
>   Dash pepper
> 1 10-ounce package frozen peas
> 1 16-ounce can tomatoes, cut up
> 1 6-ounce package Minute Spanish
>   Rice Mix
> ¼ cup sliced pitted ripe olives

On Range Top: In skillet brown chicken in hot oil. Sprinkle with a little salt, pepper, and paprika; set aside. Meanwhile, combine ground beef, ½ teaspoon salt, and dash pepper; shape into 18 tiny meatballs. Lightly brown meatballs in same skillet; set aside. Pour boiling water over peas to thaw.

In bowl combine peas, tomatoes, rice mix, olives, and 1 cup water. Arrange meatballs in 8x8x2-inch baking dish. Pour rice mixture over meatballs. Arrange chicken pieces atop rice. Micro-cook, covered, till rice and chicken are done, about 20 minutes, giving dish a quarter turn every 5 minutes. Makes 6 servings.

Make-Ahead Fruit Pies

Frozen baked pies need only several minutes micro-cooking till defrosted. Use a *non-metal* pie plate and turn the dish several times for even defrosting till pie can be cut.

Frozen unbaked two-crust pies need combination cooking. Use the microwave oven till filling is cooked; then put pie into conventional oven to brown. Do not use metal pie plate; transfer to glass pie plate if necessary. Micro-cook frozen pie till filling is thawed and fruit is tender, about 15 minutes. Meanwhile, preheat conventional oven to 450°; finish pie by browning in conventional oven till crust is golden, about 10 minutes.

Egg and Potato Casserole

A meatless main dish shown on page 2 —

> 4 eggs
> 4 medium potatoes, peeled and
>   quartered (1¼ pounds)
>   ● ● ●
> ¼ cup chopped onion
> 1 tablespoon butter *or* margarine
> 3 tablespoons all-purpose flour
> 1 8-ounce can imitation
>   sour cream
> ¾ cup shredded sharp American
>   cheese (3 ounces)
> ½ cup milk
> ½ teaspoon salt
> ⅛ teaspoon paprika
> ⅛ teaspoon pepper
>   ● ● ●
> 2 tomatoes, peeled and thinly
>   sliced
> 1 tablespoon butter *or* margarine
> ¾ cup soft bread crumbs (1 slice)
> ¼ teaspoon paprika

On Range Top: Place eggs in saucepan; cover with cold water at least 1 inch above eggs. Cover. Rapidly bring to boiling; reduce heat and keep water just below simmering 15 to 20 minutes. Cool immediately in cold water. Peel and slice; set aside.

Meanwhile, in 1½-quart casserole cover potatoes with water. Micro-cook, covered, till potatoes are tender, 12 to 15 minutes. Drain, slice, and set potatoes aside.

In glass bowl micro-cook onion in 1 tablespoon butter or margarine till tender, about 1½ minutes. Blend in flour; stir in sour cream, shredded cheese, milk, salt, ⅛ teaspoon paprika, and pepper. Micro-cook, uncovered, till cheese melts, about 1½ minutes, stirring once. Combine sauce and potatoes.

In same 1½-quart casserole layer *half* of the potato mixture. Top with egg slices and tomato slices. Spoon remaining potato mixture atop. Micro-melt 1 tablespoon butter 30 to 40 seconds; stir in crumbs and ¼ teaspoon paprika. Sprinkle crumbs atop casserole.

Micro-cook, uncovered, till heated through, about 7 minutes, turning dish twice. Let stand 3 to 5 minutes before serving. If desired, garnish with additional hard-cooked egg and tomato wedges and parsley. Serves 4.

Dovetail the cooking steps when making *Sausage-Sauced Cabbage.* While the cabbage wedges are cooking in a skillet on top of the range, prepare the sausage mixture in the micro-wave oven. This spicy meat and vegetable main dish is ready to serve in less than 15 minutes.

Sausage-Sauced Cabbage

> **1 medium head cabbage, cut in 6 wedges (1 pound)**
> **½ pound bulk Italian pork sausage**
> **½ cup chopped onion**
> **½ cup chopped green pepper**
> **1 8-ounce can tomato sauce**
> **1 8-ounce can tomatoes, cut up**
> **1 tablespoon snipped parsley**
> **2 teaspoons sugar**
> **½ teaspoon salt**
> **½ teaspoon dried oregano, crushed**

On Range Top: Cook cabbage, covered, in a 10-inch skillet in a small amount of boiling salted water till tender, 10 to 12 minutes.

Meanwhile, in glass bowl crumble sausage; add onion and green pepper. Micro-cook, covered, till meat is brown, about 5 minutes, stirring several times to break up meat. Drain off excess fat. Stir in remaining ingredients. Micro-cook, covered, till heated through, about 3 minutes, stirring once. Drain cabbage well. Arrange cabbage wedges on serving plate. Pour some sauce over cabbage. Pass remaining sauce. Makes 6 servings.

Tuna-Noodle Casserole

Frozen noodles make this casserole special—

On Range Top: In saucepan bring 6 cups water to boiling. Add one 8-ounce package frozen noodles, stirring till separated. Boil rapidly till tender, 15 to 20 minutes. Drain; set aside.

Meanwhile, in 1½-quart casserole micro-cook 1 cup chopped celery and ¼ cup chopped onion in 2 tablespoons butter *or* margarine, covered, till vegetables are tender, 3½ to 4 minutes, stirring twice. Blend in 2 tablespoons all-purpose flour. Stir one 11-ounce can con-densed Cheddar cheese soup and ¾ cup milk into mixture in casserole.

Micro-cook, uncovered, till mixture is thick-ened and bubbly, about 4 minutes, stirring after each minute. Fold in one 9¼-ounce can tuna, drained and flaked; one 2-ounce jar sliced canned pimiento, drained and chopped (¼ cup); and the cooked noodles. Micro-cook, uncovered, till heated through, 3 to 4 minutes, stirring after 2 minutes. Stir mixture, then sprinkle ¼ cup grated Parmesan cheese and ¼ cup sliced pitted ripe olives over top of noodle mixture. Makes 6 servings.

Microwave Plus the Freezer

Plan to use your freezer in conjunction with cooking in the microwave oven to help simplify menu preparations. Make foods ahead, then freeze them until you are ready for the final preparation steps in the microwave oven.

Basic Frozen Meatballs

In large bowl combine 2 beaten eggs, ⅓ cup milk, 2 cups soft bread crumbs, ⅓ cup finely chopped onion, 1½ teaspoons salt, and ⅛ teaspoon pepper. Add 2 pounds ground beef; mix well. With wet hands shape meat mixture into forty-eight 1-inch meatballs. Place on baking sheet. Cover; freeze just till frozen.

Using 24 meatballs per package, wrap in two moisture-vaporproof bags. Seal, label, and freeze. Use in Stroganoff Meatballs or Chili Meatball Supper. Makes 48 meatballs.

Chili Meatball Supper

  24 **Basic Frozen Meatballs**
   1 **16-ounce can tomatoes, cut up**
   1 **15½-ounce can red kidney beans**
   1 **12-ounce can whole kernel corn with sweet peppers**
   1 **8-ounce can tomato sauce with chopped onion**
   2 **teaspoons chili powder**
   1 **bay leaf**
   ½ **cup shredded American cheese**
   1 **cup crushed corn chips**

Place frozen meatballs in single layer in 12x 7½x2-inch baking dish. Micro-cook, covered, till thawed, about 4 minutes, rearranging meatballs after each minute. Micro-cook, covered, till done, about 6 minutes more, turning meatballs over and rearranging twice. Drain off excess fat. Add undrained tomatoes, beans, and corn; mix in tomato sauce, chili powder, and bay leaf. Micro-cook, covered, till bubbly, about 10 to 12 minutes, stirring every 3 minutes. Remove bay leaf. Serve in bowls topped with cheese and chips. Serves 6.

Stroganoff Meatballs

Thoroughly blend soup and milk into softened cream cheese for a smooth sauce—

  24 **Basic Frozen Meatballs**
   1 **3-ounce package cream cheese, cut in cubes**
   1 **10¾-ounce can condensed cream of mushroom soup**
   ¾ **cup milk**
        • • •
   2 **tablespoons catsup**
   ¼ **teaspoon dried thyme, crushed**
   ⅛ **teaspoon garlic powder**
        • • •
   ½ **cup dairy sour cream**
     Hot cooked rice or hot cooked noodles
     Snipped parsley

Place frozen meatballs in single layer in 12x 7½x2-inch baking dish. Micro-cook, covered, till thawed, about 4 minutes, rearranging meatballs after each minute. Micro-cook, covered, till done, about 6 minutes longer, turning meatballs over and rearranging them twice. Drain off excess fat.

In a 2-quart casserole soften cream cheese in microwave oven about 30 seconds. Thoroughly blend in the soup and milk. Stir in the catsup, thyme, and garlic powder. Micro-cook, covered, till cheese is melted and mixture is smooth, about 8 minutes, stirring every 2 minutes. Add the meatballs. Micro-cook, covered, till bubbly, about 5 minutes, stirring twice.

Stir a moderate amount of the hot sauce into the sour cream; return to casserole. Micro-cook, covered, just till hot, about 1 minute longer. *Do not boil.* Serve over hot cooked rice or noodles. Sprinkle with snipped parsley. Makes 4 to 6 servings.

Keep a supply of meatballs in the freezer; then ❯ when dinnertime rolls around, let the microwave oven do the quick thawing. One of the tasty dishes using the *Basic Frozen Meatballs* recipe is *Chili Meatball Supper.*

Cauliflower-Salmon Bake

Place one 10-ounce package frozen cauliflower in 2-quart glass bowl. To thaw, micro-cook, covered, 1 minute. Cut up large pieces. Micro-cook, covered, 1 minute more. Drain cauliflower and set aside.

In same bowl micro-cook ½ cup chopped onion and 1 tablespoon water till onion is tender, about 2 to 3 minutes. Stir in one 11-ounce can condensed Cheddar cheese soup and 2 tablespoons milk. Stir in one 3-ounce can chopped mushrooms, drained; 2 tablespoons snipped parsley; 1 teaspoon Worcestershire sauce; and dash cayenne. Fold in one 7¾-ounce can salmon, drained, bones and skin removed, and broken into chunks, and the cauliflower. Turn mixture into four 1-cup casseroles. Cover, seal, label, and freeze.

To serve, place frozen casseroles on microwave oven glass tray (or set casseroles on waxed paper if oven doesn't have glass tray). Micro-cook, covered, till heated through: one casserole 7 to 8 minutes, two casseroles 11 to 12 minutes, and four casseroles 12 to 13 minutes. Rearrange dishes three times. Sprinkle ¼ cup crisp rice cereal squares, coarsely crushed, atop before serving. Makes 4 servings.

Twice-Baked Potatoes

Prepare and micro-cook four medium baking potatoes following directions given for Baked Potatoes on page 38. Cut lengthwise slice from top of each potato; discard skin from slice. Reserving potato shells, scoop out inside and add to potato from slice; mash. Add 2 tablespoons butter, ½ teaspoon salt, and ⅛ teaspoon pepper. Beat in enough milk (about ½ cup) to make a stiff consistency. Stir in one 3-ounce can chopped mushrooms, drained. Pile mixture back into potato shells. Sprinkle with paprika. Wrap, seal, label, and freeze.

To serve, unwrap frozen potatoes and place in 10x6x2-inch baking dish. Micro-cook, uncovered, till potatoes are heated through, about 13 minutes for four potatoes (7 to 9 minutes for two potatoes), rearranging potatoes two or three times. Cut 2 slices Swiss cheese in half diagonally. Place cheese atop potatoes. Micro-cook 30 seconds more. Serves 4.

Italian-Style Stuffed Peppers

  6 medium green peppers
  1 pound ground beef
  ½ cup chopped onion
  1 8-ounce can tomatoes, cut up
  ¾ cup Minute Rice
  1 envelope spaghetti sauce mix
  ½ cup shredded mozzarella cheese

In 2-quart casserole micro-cook 3 cups water to boiling, about 12 minutes. Meanwhile, cut off tops of peppers; remove seeds and membrane. Add 3 peppers at a time to boiling water. Micro-cook, covered, 2 minutes. Remove; drain. Repeat. Discard water. In same casserole crumble meat. Add onion. Cook, covered, till meat is brown, about 5 minutes, stirring several times. Drain. Stir in tomatoes, rice, sauce mix, and ¾ cup water. Cook, covered, till rice is done, about 6 minutes; stir twice. Stir in cheese; fill peppers. Seal, label, and freeze in freezer container.

To serve, place frozen peppers in 8x8x2-inch baking dish. Micro-cook, covered, 2 minutes. Let stand 2 minutes. Cook till filling is hot, 18 to 19 minutes; rearrange every 5 minutes. Sprinkle tops with Parmesan cheese. Serves 6.

Barbecue Sandwiches

In 2-quart glass bowl combine two 10¾-ounce cans condensed tomato soup, ½ cup finely chopped onion, ¼ cup water, 3 tablespoons vinegar, 2 tablespoons sugar, 2 tablespoons Worcestershire sauce, 1 tablespoon prepared mustard, and ¼ teaspoon bottled hot pepper sauce. Micro-cook, covered, till bubbly, about 8 minutes, stirring twice. Stir in 1 pound cooked pork *or* beef, chilled and sliced *very* thin (3 cups). Seal, label, and freeze in three pint-size freezer containers.

To serve, place contents of one container in 1-quart casserole. Micro-cook, covered, 2 minutes; let stand 2 minutes. Continue cooking till thawed and hot, 8 to 10 minutes more, stirring every 2 minutes. *Or,* for two containers place contents in 2-quart casserole. Micro-cook, covered, 6 minutes; let stand 2 minutes. Micro-cook 8 minutes more, stirring every 2 minutes. Serve on split hard rolls or buns. Makes 3 or 4 sandwiches per pint container.

Oriental Beef Casserole

In 1½-quart casserole crumble 1 pound ground beef. Add ¼ cup *each* chopped celery, onion, and green pepper. Micro-cook, covered, till meat is brown and vegetables are tender, about 5 minutes, stirring several times. Drain off fat. Stir in 1 cup water. Micro-cook, uncovered, till mixture bubbles, about 3 minutes; stir once. Combine 2 tablespoons cornstarch, 1 teaspoon sugar, and ¼ teaspoon ground ginger; blend in ¼ cup soy sauce and 2 tablespoons water. Stir into beef mixture.

Micro-cook, uncovered, till thickened and bubbly, about 1½ minutes, stirring twice. Stir in one 8½-ounce can bamboo shoots, drained, and one 6-ounce package frozen pea pods, thawed. Turn mixture into four 12-ounce casseroles. Cover, seal, label, and freeze.

To serve, place frozen casseroles, covered with waxed paper, in microwave oven. Micro-cook 2 minutes; let stand 2 minutes. Micro-cook till hot: one casserole 5 minutes, two casseroles 10 minutes, and four casseroles 17 minutes. Give dishes half turns three times and rearrange once. Before serving, sprinkle chow mein noodles over tops. Serves 4.

Coffee-Mallow Tortoni

  1 cup tiny marshmallows
  ⅓ cup milk
  1 teaspoon instant coffee crystals
  ¼ cup chopped almonds, toasted*
  2 egg whites
  ½ teaspoon vanilla
  2 tablespoons sugar
  ½ cup whipping cream

In 4-cup glass measure combine marshmallows and milk. Micro-cook, uncovered, till marshmallows begin to melt, about 1½ minutes. Stir to blend. If marshmallows are not all melted, micro-cook a few seconds more. Stir in coffee crystals; chill till partially set. Stir in nuts (*see tip, page 36, for toasting). Beat whites and vanilla till soft peaks form; add sugar, beating to stiff peaks. Whip cream till soft peaks form. Fold whites and cream into coffee mixture. Freeze till firm in muffin pans lined with paper bake cups. If desired, top with maraschino cherry halves. Serves 6 to 8.

Beanless Chili

In 3-quart casserole crumble 2 pounds ground beef. Add 1 cup chopped onion; ½ cup chopped green pepper; 1 clove garlic, minced; and 1½ teaspoons salt. Micro-cook, covered, till meat is brown, about 10 minutes, stirring several times to break up meat. Drain off fat.

Stir in one 28-ounce can tomatoes, cut up; one 10½-ounce can tomato purée; ½ cup water; one 4-ounce can mild green chili peppers, drained, seeded, and chopped; 1 tablespoon chili powder; 1 teaspoon sugar; ½ teaspoon dried basil, crushed; and ½ teaspoon ground cumin. Micro-cook, covered, 10 minutes; stir three times. Seal, label, and freeze in two 1-quart *or* four 1-pint freezer containers.

To serve, place 1 quart frozen mixture in 1½-quart casserole. Micro-cook, covered, 2 minutes; let stand 2 minutes. Cook, covered, till hot, about 16 minutes, stirring three times to break up meat. *Or*, place 1 pint frozen mixture in 1-quart casserole. Micro-cook, covered, 2 minutes; let stand 2 minutes. Cook, covered, till hot, about 9 minutes, stirring twice. Serve in bowls over hot cooked rice. Makes 8 servings.

Date-Rice Dessert

A frosty fix-up for pudding mix shown on page 74—

  ½ cup Minute Rice
  1 3- or 3¼-ounce package
    regular vanilla pudding mix
  2 cups milk
  ½ cup snipped pitted dates
  ½ teaspoon shredded lemon peel
  1 4½-ounce container frozen whipped
    dessert topping, thawed (2 cups)

In a 4-cup glass measure combine the rice, pudding mix, and ¼ teaspoon salt. Stir in milk. Micro-cook, uncovered, 3 minutes. Stir. Micro-cook, uncovered, till mixture thickens and bubbles, 3 to 4 minutes, stirring every 30 seconds. Fold in dates and peel. Cool to room temperature without stirring. Fold in topping. Turn into 10x6x2-inch baking dish. Cover and freeze. Before serving, remove from freezer and place in refrigerator about 45 minutes. Cut in squares to serve. Or, thaw at room temperature 45 minutes; spoon into sherbet dishes. Trim with a thin lemon slice, if desired. Serves 6.

Microwave Plus the Barbecue

Speed up the cooking time of some barbecued foods by using the microwave oven. Or, use the microwave oven to reheat leftover charcoaled foods. By grilling extras over the coals, you can have a barbecue meal stored away for another meal without heating the grill.

Spicy Barbecued Ribs

    ¼ cup finely chopped onion
    2 tablespoons butter *or* margarine
    ½ cup chili sauce
    ⅓ cup vinegar
    ¼ cup packed brown sugar
      Dash bottled hot pepper sauce
    3 pounds pork spareribs

In glass bowl micro-cook onion in butter till tender, about 1½ minutes. Stir in chili sauce, vinegar, sugar, pepper sauce, and 1 teaspoon salt. Cut ribs in serving-size pieces. Arrange in 12x7½x2-inch baking dish. Micro-cook, covered, for 20 minutes, rearranging ribs after 10 minutes. Transfer ribs to barbecue grill. Grill over *medium* coals till done, about 15 minutes. Brush often with sauce and turn ribs over occasionally. Makes 3 or 4 servings.

Mustard Barbecued Ribs

    ¼ cup prepared mustard
    2 tablespoons molasses
    2 tablespoons Worcestershire sauce
      Dash bottled hot pepper sauce
    3 pounds pork spareribs
    1 12-ounce can beer (1½ cups)
    1 small onion, quartered

Combine first four ingredients; set aside. Cut ribs in serving-size pieces. Arrange in 12x7½x 2-inch baking dish; add beer, onion, 1 teaspoon salt, and dash pepper. Micro-cook, covered, 20 minutes, rearranging ribs after 10 minutes. Transfer ribs to barbecue grill. Grill over *medium* coals 10 minutes. Brush sauce over ribs. Grill 5 minutes more; brush with sauce and turn ribs over occasionally. Serves 3 or 4.

Lemon Marinated Chuck

    1 2½- to 3-pound beef chuck roast,
        cut 1½ inches thick
    1 teaspoon grated lemon peel
    ½ cup lemon juice
    ¼ cup cooking oil
    2 tablespoons chopped onion
    1 tablespoon sugar
    1 teaspoon Worcestershire sauce
    1 teaspoon Dijon-style mustard

Score fat edges of meat. Place in 12x7½x2-inch baking dish, trimming meat to fit dish, if necessary. Combine remaining ingredients, 1½ teaspoons salt, and ⅛ teaspoon pepper. Pour over meat. Cover; refrigerate 12 hours or overnight, turning meat several times. Micro-cook meat in marinade, covered, 15 to 20 minutes, turning meat over once. Transfer meat to barbecue grill. Grill over *medium-hot* coals about 5 minutes on *each* side for rare to medium-rare. Brush often with marinade. To serve, slice thinly across grain. Serves 6 to 8.

Barbecued Marinated Chicken

    1 2-pound ready-to-cook
        broiler-fryer chicken
    ½ cup dry sherry
    2 tablespoons honey
    1 tablespoon soy sauce
    1 teaspoon dry mustard
    ½ teaspoon ground ginger
    ¼ teaspoon paprika

RECIPE FOR **2**

Halve chicken lengthwise; place in shallow baking dish. Combine remaining ingredients; pour over chicken. Cover; refrigerate 4 to 6 hours, occasionally spooning marinade over.

Remove chicken, reserving marinade. Arrange chicken, skin side up, in 10x6x2-inch baking dish. Micro-cook, covered, 18 minutes, giving dish a quarter turn every 3 minutes. Transfer chicken to barbecue grill. Grill over *hot* coals till done, about 10 minutes. Brush occasionally with marinade and turn chicken until evenly browned. Makes 2 servings.

A perfect outdoor meal for two includes *Barbe-cued Marinated Chicken* served with slices of garlic toast and a unique relish salad. For each serving of salad, use a green pepper cup as a holder for other relishes—carrot and celery sticks, olives, and radishes.

Barbecued Hawaiian Chicken

>   1 3-pound ready-to-cook broiler
>   fryer chicken, cut up
> ¼ cup apricot preserves
> ¼ cup Russian salad dressing
>   with honey
>   2 tablespoons dry onion soup mix

Arrange chicken, skin side up, in 10x6x2-inch baking dish. Micro-cook, covered, 15 minutes, giving dish a quarter turn every 3 minutes. Transfer chicken to barbecue grill and grill over *hot* coals for 5 minutes. Combine the preserves, salad dressing, and soup mix. Brush mixture over chicken. Grill till chicken is done, about 10 minutes more. Brush occasionally with preserves mixture and turn chicken until evenly browned. Makes 4 servings.

Snappy Barbecued Pork Chops

In 2-cup glass measure combine one 8-ounce can tomato sauce, ¼ cup molasses, ¼ cup water, 2 tablespoons vinegar, 1 tablespoon Worcestershire sauce, 2 teaspoons instant minced onion, 2 teaspoons dry mustard, 1 teaspoon salt, ¼ teaspoon chili powder, and dash pepper. Micro-cook, uncovered, till bubbly, about 3½ minutes. Arrange 4 rib *or* loin pork chops cut 1 inch thick in 8x8x2-inch baking dish. Micro-cook, covered, 12 to 15 minutes, giving dish a quarter turn every 3 minutes.

Transfer chops to barbecue grill. Grill over *medium* coals till done, about 15 minutes. Brush frequently with sauce and turn chops over occasionally. Micro-heat remaining sauce, about 30 seconds; pass with chops. Serves 4.

Special Microwave Features

*M*any microwave appliances have special features available. Some models have a defrost feature while others have several cooking speeds, making slower cooking possible. Special browning dishes and infrared browning units are two other optional helps. Check this section for ways to use these features.

Vegetable-Stuffed Pork Rolls

½ cup shredded carrot
½ cup finely chopped onion
½ cup finely chopped green pepper
½ cup grated Parmesan cheese
¼ teaspoon dried thyme, crushed
6 pork tenderloin pieces
    (about 4 ounces each)
1 cup beef broth
4 teaspoons cornstarch
1 2-ounce can chopped mushrooms,
    drained
¼ teaspoon Kitchen Bouquet

In a 1-quart casserole combine carrot, onion, green pepper, ¼ cup water, and ¼ teaspoon salt. Micro-cook, covered, on *high* setting till crisp-tender, about 4 minutes. Drain thoroughly. Stir in cheese and thyme; set aside.

Pound each piece of pork to a piece measuring 8x5 inches. Season with salt and pepper. Spread about ¼ *cup* of the vegetable mixture on *each* piece. Roll up, beginning with short side; secure with string or wooden picks. Place meat rolls in 12x7½x2-inch baking dish. Pour beef broth over. Micro-cook, covered, on *simmer* (medium) setting till meat is tender, about 30 minutes, turning rolls over and rearranging once. Transfer meat to serving plate. Remove strings or picks. Keep hot.

Strain 1 cup of the juices into a 2-cup glass measure. Stir 2 tablespoons cold water into cornstarch; stir into measuring cup along with mushrooms. Micro-cook, uncovered, on *high* setting, till thickened and bubbly, about 2 minutes, stirring every 30 seconds. Stir in the Kitchen Bouquet and season with salt and pepper. Serve over pork rolls. Makes 6 servings.

Burgundy Pot Roast

½ cup chopped onion
½ teaspoon instant beef
    bouillon granules
¼ cup Burgundy
1 tablespoon Worcestershire sauce
1 3-pound beef chuck roast
4 teaspoons cornstarch

In 2-cup glass measure combine onion and ⅓ cup water. Micro-cook, uncovered, on *high* setting till tender, about 2 minutes; do not drain. Stir in bouillon granules. Add Burgundy, Worcestershire sauce, ½ teaspoon salt, and ⅛ teaspoon pepper. Place meat in 12x7½x2-inch baking dish. Pour wine mixture over.

Micro-cook, covered, on *defrost* setting for 1½ hours, turning meat over in dish and giving dish half turns every 30 minutes. Remove meat to platter; keep covered. Pour pan drippings into a 2-cup glass measure; skim off fat. Stir 2 tablespoons cold water into cornstarch; stir into meat liquid. Micro-cook, uncovered, on *high* setting 1 minute; stir. Cook till thickened and bubbly, 1 to 2 minutes, stirring every 30 seconds. Serves 6.

Beef-Barley Vegetable Soup

8 ounces beef chuck, cut in small
    pieces
1 16-ounce can tomatoes, cut up
1 cup chopped celery
½ cup chopped onion
2 tablespoons quick-cooking barley
1 tablespoon Worcestershire sauce
¼ teaspoon chili powder
1 8¾-ounce can whole kernel corn

In 3-quart casserole combine all ingredients *except* corn. Stir in 4 cups water, ¾ teaspoon salt, and ⅛ teaspoon pepper. Micro-cook, covered, on *high* setting, till mixture boils, about 15 minutes. Cook, covered, on *defrost* setting 1 hour; stir every 20 minutes. Stir in undrained corn. Cook, covered, on *high* setting until hot, about 1 minute more. Makes 8 servings.

Chicken Country Captain

In a 3-quart casserole combine ¼ cup *each* chopped onion and green pepper; 1 small clove garlic, crushed; and 2 tablespoons butter. Micro-cook, covered, on *high* setting till vegetables are tender, about 2 minutes. Stir in one 16-ounce can tomatoes, cut up; 2 tablespoons dried currants; 2 tablespoons snipped parsley; 2 teaspoons curry powder; 1 teaspoon salt; ½ teaspoon ground mace; and ⅛ teaspoon pepper. Add one 2½- to 3-pound ready-to-cook broiler-fryer chicken, cut up, stirring gently to coat with sauce. Micro-cook, covered, on *defrost* setting till chicken is done, about 35 to 45 minutes, stirring every 10 minutes. Remove chicken to serving platter; keep hot.

Skim off excess fat. Stir 2 tablespoons cold water into 1 tablespoon cornstarch; stir into sauce. Micro-cook, uncovered, on *high* setting till mixture thickens and bubbles, about 3 minutes, stirring after each minute. Serve with chicken and hot cooked rice. Serves 4.

Orange Baked Cornish Hens

2 1-pound ready-to-cook Rock
    Cornish game hens
¼ cup chopped onion
2 tablespoons butter *or* margarine
1½ cups dry bread cubes (2 slices)
2 tablespoons chopped walnuts
1 teaspoon grated orange peel
2 tablespoons orange juice
    Paprika
1 tablespoon orange marmalade
1 teaspoon bottled steak sauce

RECIPE FOR **2**

Season inside of hens with salt and pepper. In 4-cup glass measure micro-cook onion in butter, uncovered, on *high* setting till onion is tender, about 1½ minutes. Stir in bread, nuts, peel, and ¼ teaspoon salt. Toss with juice. Stuff birds with mixture. Tie legs together. Place, breast side down, in 10x6x2-inch baking dish. Sprinkle with paprika. Micro-cook, uncovered, on *high* setting 10 minutes. Turn breast up; sprinkle with paprika. Cook, uncovered, on *roast* (medium-high) setting till done, about 10 minutes. Mix last 2 ingredients. Brush on birds; micro-cook, uncovered, on *high* setting 1 minute. Let stand 5 minutes. Serves 2.

Cake-Style Brownies

½ cup butter *or* margarine
3 tablespoons unsweetened
    cocoa powder
1 cup all-purpose flour
1 cup sugar
½ teaspoon baking soda
¼ cup buttermilk *or* sour milk
1 slightly beaten egg
1 teaspoon vanilla
Fast Fudge Frosting

In 4-cup glass measure combine butter, cocoa powder, and ½ cup water. Micro-cook, uncovered, on *high* setting till boiling, about 3 minutes, stirring once to blend. Set aside. Stir together the flour, sugar, soda, and ¼ teaspoon salt; stir in the buttermilk, egg, and vanilla. Stir in cocoa mixture. Pour into greased 12x7½x2-inch baking dish. Micro-cook, uncovered, on *roast* (medium-high) setting for 7½ minutes, giving dish half turns every 2 minutes. (Top will be slightly moist.) Cool completely. Frost with Fast Fudge Frosting. Makes 28 bars.

Fast Fudge Frosting: Combine 2½ cups sifted powdered sugar, ¼ cup unsweetened cocoa powder, and ⅛ teaspoon salt. Add 3 tablespoons boiling water, 3 tablespoons softened butter, and 1 teaspoon vanilla. Blend well.

Lemon Cottage Cheesecake

For crust, in 8x1½-inch round glass baking dish micro-melt 2 tablespoons butter on *high* setting 30 to 40 seconds. Stir in ¾ cup finely crushed zwieback and ¼ cup sifted powdered sugar. Reserve 1 tablespoon for top; press remainder evenly in bottom of dish. Set aside.

Sieve 2 cups well-drained cream-style cottage cheese into mixing bowl. Add 4 eggs, 1 cup granulated sugar, 1 cup whipping cream, ¼ cup all-purpose flour, 1 teaspoon grated lemon peel, 3 tablespoons lemon juice, ½ teaspoon vanilla, and ¼ teaspoon salt. Beat just till combined. (*Or*, omit sieving and combine all ingredients in blender container; blend just till smooth.) Pour into crust. Top with reserved crumbs. Micro-cook, uncovered, on *defrost* setting till nearly set in center, 21 to 23 minutes; give dish a half turn after 10 minutes. Chill. Cut in wedges. Serves 8 to 10.

Horseradish-Stuffed Rump Roast

Use a regular meat thermometer if a microwave thermometer is not available. But you must take the meat out of the oven to test and remove the regular thermometer before returning meat to oven—

> **1 5-ounce jar prepared horseradish**
> **2 cloves garlic, minced**
> **1 5-pound boned and rolled**
> **beef rump roast**
> **1 teaspoon beef-flavored**
> **gravy base**
> **⅓ cup cold water**
> **3 tablespoons all-purpose flour**
> **Salt and pepper**

Combine horseradish and the 2 cloves of garlic. Unroll roast; make lengthwise cut through thick part of roast, going to, but not through other side. Spread cut surfaces with the horseradish mixture. Reroll roast and tie securely with string. Rub roast with a cut clove of garlic, if desired.

Place roast, fat side down, on inverted saucer in 12x7½x2-inch baking dish. Micro-cook, uncovered, on *roast* (medium-high) setting for 30 minutes; give dish half turns every 10 minutes.

Turn meat, fat side up, and change setting on microwave oven to *simmer* (medium) setting. Micro-cook, uncovered, till microwave thermometer registers 140°, about 25 to 30 minutes; give dish half turns every 10 minutes. Remove roast; cover with foil and let stand 20 minutes before carving. (Temperature will increase to 160° during standing time for medium-done beef.)

Pour off pan drippings into a 4-cup glass measure. Skim off excess fat. To drippings add enough water to make 1½ cups and the beef-flavored gravy base; set aside.

About 10 minutes before serving, stir ⅓ cup cold water into the flour. Add to mixture in glass measure. Micro-cook, uncovered, on *high* setting 1 minute; stir. Micro-cook till thickened and bubbly, about 3½ to 4 minutes, stirring after each minute. Season to taste with salt and pepper. Serve with meat. Serves 10.

◄ **Slower cooking** of less tender cuts of meat is possible when you have a microwave appliance that has various cooking speeds. *Microwave Beef Stew* is cooked on the simmer (medium) setting for a total of about 70 minutes.

Microwave Beef Stew

Coat 1 pound beef chuck, cut in ¾-inch cubes, with a mixture of 2 tablespoons all-purpose flour, 1 teaspoon salt, and dash pepper. In 3-quart casserole combine one 10¾-ounce can condensed tomato soup; 1 soup can water; 1 cup chopped onion; 1 teaspoon instant beef bouillon granules; 1 teaspoon dried savory, crushed; and ¼ teaspoon garlic powder. Stir in seasoned cubes of meat.

Micro-cook, covered, on *simmer* (medium) setting for 35 minutes, stirring after 20 minutes. Stir in 4 medium carrots, cut in ½-inch pieces; micro-cook, covered, on *simmer* setting 5 minutes. Stir in 3 medium potatoes, peeled and cut in 1-inch cubes; micro-cook, covered, on *simmer* setting till vegetables are tender, about 25 to 30 minutes, stirring three times. Stir ½ cup cold water into 2 tablespoons cornstarch; blend into meat mixture. Micro-cook, uncovered, on *high* setting till thickened and bubbly, about 3 minutes, stirring after each minute. Season to taste. Serve in bowls. Makes 4 servings.

Chicken Divan

Do all cooking on high or cook setting—

Place two 8- *or* 10-ounce packages frozen cut asparagus side by side in 12x7½x2-inch baking dish. Add 2 tablespoons water. Micro-cook, covered, till tender, 10 to 12 minutes, separating pieces with fork after 6 minutes. Drain well on paper toweling. Return to same dish.

Blend one 10½-ounce can condensed cream of chicken soup, 1 teaspoon Worcestershire sauce, and dash ground nutmeg. Pour *half* over asparagus in 12x7½x2-inch baking dish. Using ½ cup grated Parmesan cheese, sprinkle *one-third* of the cheese over sauce on asparagus. Top with 2 cups cut up cooked chicken and remaining soup mixture. Sprinkle with another *third* of the cheese. Micro-cook, uncovered, till hot, about 6 to 8 minutes. Remove from oven.

Under Infrared Browning Unit: Preheat unit for 2 minutes. Meanwhile, whip ½ cup whipping cream to soft peaks; fold in ½ cup mayonnaise. Spread over chicken mixture. Sprinkle with remaining cheese. Brown on bottom shelf about 6 inches from infrared unit till top is golden, about 4 minutes. Serves 6 to 8.

Surprise Cream Pie

Do all cooking on high or cook setting—

Prepare *Crumb Crust*: In 9-inch glass pie plate micro-melt 5 tablespoons butter, about 45 seconds. Stir in 1¼ cups finely crushed graham crackers and ¼ cup sugar. Press over bottom and sides of pie plate. Micro-cook, uncovered, 2 minutes, turning dish after 1 minute.

Break up two 1-ounce milk chocolate candy bars and arrange over hot crust; spread till smooth. Set crust aside.

In 4-cup glass measure combine one 4½- *or* 5-ounce package *regular* vanilla pudding mix and 3 cups milk. Micro-cook, uncovered, 3 minutes. Stir. Micro-cook, uncovered, till pudding thickens and bubbles, about 2 to 3 minutes more, stirring after each minute. Stir *half* of the hot pudding into 2 slightly beaten egg yolks. Return to hot mixture. Micro-cook 1 minute more. Pour into prepared crust.

In small bowl beat 2 egg whites with ½ teaspoon vanilla and ¼ teaspoon cream of tartar till soft peaks form. Gradually add ¼ cup sugar, beating till stiff peaks form. Spread atop pie, sealing to edges of crust.

Under Infrared Browning Unit: Do not preheat unit. Brown pie about 3 to 4 minutes, turning pie for even browning as necessary. Cool.

Tropical French Toast

    1 egg
    ¼ cup milk
    ⅛ teaspoon salt
    Dash ground cinnamon
    ½ ripe small banana, cut up
    4 ¾-inch-thick slices French bread
    1 tablespoon butter *or* margarine
    Maple syrup *or* tart jelly

RECIPE FOR **2**

In blender container combine egg, milk, salt, and cinnamon; blend till smooth. Add banana pieces; blend till smooth. Pour mixture into shallow dish. Dip both sides of bread slices in mixture. Meanwhile, heat *browning skillet or platter* in microwave oven on *high* setting for 3½ minutes. Add butter to dish, lightly greasing surface. Place bread on dish. Micro-cook, uncovered, on *high* setting 45 seconds. Turn toast over; micro-cook 45 seconds more. Serve with syrup or jelly. Serves 2.

Veal Parmesan

An Italian-style dish shown on page 74—

Cut 1 pound boneless veal sirloin steak into four serving size pieces. Pound meat till ¼ inch thick. Combine ¼ cup finely crushed saltine crackers, ¼ cup grated Parmesan cheese, and dash pepper. Dip veal in 1 beaten egg, and then dip in the crumb mixture; set aside.

Heat *browning skillet or platter* in microwave oven on *high* setting for 2 minutes. Place 2 pieces of the meat on dish; micro-cook, uncovered, till brown on one side, about 1½ minutes. Turn meat over; micro-cook till other side of meat is browned, about 1½ minutes longer. Transfer meat to a 12x7½x2-inch baking dish. Repeat browning with remaining meat.

Combine one 8-ounce can pizza sauce and ½ teaspoon sugar; pour over meat in baking dish. Micro-cook, covered, on *high* setting till meat is done and sauce is heated through, about 7 minutes, giving dish a quarter turn every 2 minutes and rearranging meat once. Sprinkle with 1 cup shredded mozzarella cheese. Micro-cook, uncovered, till cheese melts, about 1 minute. Garnish with parsley. Makes 4 servings.

Mushroom Burgers

    1 beaten egg
    2 tablespoons milk
    2 teaspoons instant minced onion
    ¾ cup soft bread crumbs
    1 2-ounce can chopped
        mushrooms, drained
    1 tablespoon bottled steak sauce
    1 teaspoon salt
    Dash pepper
    1½ pounds ground beef

RECIPE FOR **2**

In bowl combine egg, milk, and onion; let stand 2 minutes. Stir in crumbs, mushrooms, steak sauce, salt, and pepper. Add beef; mix well. Shape into 6 patties, each ¾ inch thick. Wrap in moisture-vaporproof material in packets of two. Seal, label, and freeze. To serve, heat *browning skillet or platter* in microwave oven on *high* setting for 6 minutes. Place two frozen meat patties on hot dish. Micro-cook, covered, on *high* setting 4 minutes. Turn patties over. Micro-cook, covered, till desired doneness, about 3 minutes longer. Makes 2 servings.

INDEX
A-B